The Politics of Bureaucratic Reform

THE POLITICS OF BUREAUCRATIC REFORM

The Case of the California State Employment Service

MICHAEL B. PRESTON

University of Illinois Press

Urbana and Chicago

This book is printed on acid-free paper.

Library of Congress Cataloging in Publication Data

Preston, Michael B.
    The politics of bureaucratic reform.

    Bibliography: p.
    Includes index.
    1. California. State Employment Service. 2. Adminis-
trative agencies—California—Reorganization.
I. Title.
HD5876.C2P73   1984   353.97940083'3'06   83-6980
ISBN 0-252-01048-5

To
Mary M. Preston

We trained hard, but it seemed that every time we were beginning to form up into teams we would be reorganized. I was to learn later in life that we tend to meet any new situation by reorganizing, and a wonderful method it is for creating the illusion of progress which produces confusion, inefficiency, and demoralization.

—Petronius Arbiter, 201 B.C.

Contents

Preface

This book grew out of my interest in studying manpower politics in Oakland, California, in the late 1960s and early 1970s. Like many other young political scientists at that time, I was extremely optimistic about government's ability to formulate and implement policies that would improve the lives of disadvantaged citizens. While the study of manpower policy in Oakland originally seemed to be an exciting intellectual task, I later came to the conclusion that the study of manpower policy would best be studied in a broader political context.

The agency that I decided to study was the California State Employment Service (CSES). It seemed clear to me that one of the most important things our disadvantaged citizens needed was access to more employment opportunities. At that time, as now, the CSES was the key manpower agency in the state. However, the agency was under heavy criticism from people both inside and outside of government for its inability to serve the disadvantaged. Thus, in an attempt to make the agency more responsive to the needs of this group, political officials called for agency reform. Yet, as most students of bureaucracy are aware, to reform an agency that has been in existence for over thirty years is difficult. Because the problem of reform had both personal and intellectual significance for me, I decided to study the effectiveness of administrative reorganization and decentralization as instruments of social and institutional change.

When I began this study, I did it believing that reorganization was an important area of academic inquiry. Events over the last thirteen years have given even more substance to that belief. I am grateful to the many government employees in the CSES (now California State Job Service) who originally participated in this study, and I am especially appreciative of those who kept me informed about the changes in the late 1970s and early

1980s. Much of the material in this study is based on information gathered in interviews with these employees, which I conducted over a five-year period, from 1968 to 1973. Data for the remainder of the 1970s and early 1980s were gathered through interviews and agency newsletters. Quotations from all these interviews are based on notes in my possession.

Philip Monypenny, Fred Wirt, and Tom Anton read drafts of this study and provided me with many valuable suggestions. I am especially indebted to my friend Aaron Wildavsky, who supervised my doctoral dissertation, on which this book is based. Anna Merritt has been an enormous help in editing the manuscript. Finally, a special debt of gratitude is owed to Jean Baker and the staff of the Institute of Government and Public Affairs for their assistance in typing the various drafts of this book.

Introduction

This book is about the politics of bureaucratic reform in public agencies. The reorganization of the California State Employment Service is used to illustrate four critical issues in public administration: (1) the theoretical implications of organizational reform; (2) why reforms are instituted and how they are linked to the political process; (3) the strategies used to implement reform in public organizations; and (4) the effect of reform on an agency's personnel, clientele, and external environment.

The study of bureaucratic reform has taken on increased importance in recent years for two basic reasons. For one, there is growing concern with the abuses of bureaucratic authority. For another, citizens and politicians alike are questioning the growth and expansion of federal activities. The abuses of bureaucratic authority have threatened the freedom of individual citizens and contributed to growing distrust of all government; bureaucratic growth and the expansion of federal activities into vast new areas have raised questions about the costs and control of big government. Together, they have led to severe criticism of the federal bureaucracy by people both inside and outside of government.

As a result, presidents and other elected officials have made the unresponsiveness and growth of bureaucracy a key issue in their efforts to get elected. Once in office, they have used various means to bring about bureaucratic change. For example, Presidents Richard Nixon, Gerald Ford, and Jimmy Carter all tried reorganization and the reform of programs and procedures to bring about more bureaucratic responsiveness. Nixon attempted to short-circuit the federal bureaucracy by devolving power to the local level through his revenue-sharing concept. Carter used reform of the civil service in an attempt to make career bureaucrats more responsive to presidential direction. As governor, Ronald Reagan relied heavily on reorganization, budget cuts, and procedural reforms to control bureaucratic costs and expansion. As president, he is again trying to control the bureaucracy, although this time he is relying more on deep budgetary cuts and procedural changes than on formal reorganization.

In public agencies bureaucrats are aware that the election of a new political executive always presages change in priorities and in accustomed bureaucratic operations. Change is anticipated by those involved because they know that reform of public administrative agencies is deeply embedded in the political process. While such reform is seen as a virtue by some, this view is not likely to be shared by those who work in the affected public agencies, for a change in political leadership at the top is likely to lead to instability at the bottom. Such was the case in California in 1968 when state political leaders decided to reform the Employment Service. The governor who initiated the reform was Ronald Reagan. There is a great deal of consistency in what Reagan did as governor and what he is currently doing as president to control the expansion and growth of bureaucracy.

This book describes and analyzes how California state political leaders attempted to reform a state bureaucracy—the Employment Service (now known as the Job Service). The limitations of case studies to generalize about political phenomena are well known. But one must be able to describe before one can analyze. In addition, there are several reasons why California's experience is not entirely unique.

First, California is the largest of the ten big industrial states and as such has a large and diversified population. Political trends and changes appear in California and New York earlier than in most states.

Second, California is a growth state. For example, during 1979 California's economy generated 395,000 new jobs. Employment averaged 10,285,000 compared with 9,890,000 in 1978, a growth rate of 4.0 percent. This compares with a national job growth rate in 1979 of 2.7 percent (2.6 percent excluding California). Indeed, from 1974 to 1979, of the ten largest industrial states, California was second only to Texas in the growth of its labor force (Texas, 21.3 percent; California, 20.6 percent).[1]

Third, California has a reputation for being a state with innovative leaders. Frequently new programs are initiated there before they are tried at the federal level. Some of these innovations are detailed in this study.

Fourth, the reform of the Employment Service involved over 10,000 employees in field, regional, and central offices. In 1968 the budget for all social programs in the state was over $600 million. The budget for the Employment Service alone in 1978–79 was $414.5 million and in 1980–81, $700.8 million. In other words, the budget of the California Employment Service is more than the total budget of some states. Indeed, President Reagan is fond of saying that as governor he held the second highest executive job in the country.

Fifth, California's political leaders tend to become national leaders and carry with them most of the same views they held at the state level. For example, in 1967 Reagan was elected governor. His first speech as governor was a forecast of events to come for the bureaucracy: "We are going to squeeze and cut and trim until we reduce the cost of government."[2] His first attempt to control the bureaucracy was a hiring freeze and a 10 percent spending cut in state agencies. One of his next major initiatives (partially forced on him by the Democratically controlled state legislature) was the reform of the state Employment Service. During his second term, in 1974, in an attempt to meet shifting federal priorities, the department's budget was again cut by 21.7 percent, although most cuts were absorbed because of a hiring freeze he had instituted earlier.

As president, Reagan's attempt to control bureaucracy and the cost of government is still being felt in the halls of the California bureaucracy. For example, the budgetary reductions of $35.2 billion that he proposed for 1982 had a direct impact on the Job Service in California and the nation and reduced efforts to serve those most in need. Indeed, his entitlement cuts for fiscal year 1982–84 total $43.8 billion, and most are in the area of discretionary social spending. As a result of his recent budget cuts, the Job Service in California faced one of its most severe financial crises—a budget cut of $18 million.

In order to cover the deficit, staff positions were reduced by 21 percent. This meant a loss of 710.2 positions out of 9,570.

Other items slashed substantially or eliminated included the reduction or elimination of training programs, new accounting systems, subscriptions, business cards, field office manager meetings, seminars, and the funding of California Automation Service Team (CAST) from contingent funds. These cuts were designed to save $4.4 million. Other savings were to come from reduced travel, lower utility bills, a freeze on purchases of communication equipment, and cutbacks on conferences. In effect, the service was asked to do more with less. Another important thing to note is that these cuts always seem to come when the demand for services is high.

The impact of federal budgetary cutbacks on the Employment Service was substantial. In 1978–79 the total budget was $414,500,000, of which $354.0 million (85.4 percent) were federal funds; state funds totaled $60.5 million (14.6 percent). In contrast, the budget in 1980–81 was $700 million, of which $491 million were federal funds (70.1 percent), and $209.2 million were state funds (29.9 percent). Thus by 1980–81 federal funds had been reduced by 15.3 percent, though state funds had increased by almost the same amount (see Appendix B). However, the increase in state funds went for state priorities, which meant that federally funded programs were declining at a time when more people were unemployed. The important thing to note here is that Reagan's attempts to control the bureaucracy have moved from the statehouse to the White House.

It should also be stressed that this is an empirical study that covers an unusually long period, 1968–81. This affords a somewhat unique opportunity to view changes and consequences from a broad perspective. In many respects, this is not merely a study of the politics of bureaucratic reform; it is also a study of bureaucratic resiliency. The study shows how civil servants everywhere try to cope with the ebb and flow of political events.

This study started out with the assumption that bureaucratic reform is concerned with the twin gods of economy and efficiency. A systematic study of reform proved this assumption to be incorrect. Reform, it turns out, is political. Its primary goal is to "shake up" the bureaucracy by altering the distribution of power and influence in the system. Stated differently, reform is a means used by some to deny access to others. It should be pointed out that the political competition model suggested here is only one of three models used to explain the processes and causes of governmental reorganization. The other two describe reorganization as: (1) diffused innovation and (2) adaptation to modernization. Each of these models utilizes a unique conceptual lens to explain why reorganizations occur. Some of the strengths and weaknesses of these models are discussed in Chapter 1.

Bureaucracies are primarily concerned with the implementation of public policy. When programs fail, a normal tendency is to blame failure on the bureaucracy. And while it may be true that most bureaucrats resist change to protect their own self-interest, we argue here that their mode of behavior is determined by two fundamental flaws in the policymaking process in the United States. The first evolves from the necessity for policymakers to obtain majority support to pass legislation. To achieve this support they write laws with something for everyone and leave to the bureaucrats the task of implementing legislation that is ambiguous, too broad in scope, and often contradictory in its mandates. Second, policymakers tend to take an existing instrument (a government agency) and use it regardless of the similarities between its present function and the new uses to which it is to be put. In Chapter 2 we show that a large part of bureaucratic behavior is a by-product of the flaws that exist in the national political arena.

In the 1960s the federal government's intervention in such areas as health, education, welfare, poverty, and manpower led to conflicts—which persist to this day—over state and federal roles in determining policies in these areas. For example, reform of the California Federal-State Employment Service put the state in direct conflict with the federal bureaucracy. That conflict, we argue, is part of a much broader issue in American politics—the fluctuating patterns of power between federal and state governments over who should set the standards and policies for the states. In Chapter 3 we illustrate why states do not always lose in the power play that results when local conditions lead them to depart from federally prescribed paths. In fact, the

California experience indicates that, despite the seemingly unlimited power of the federal government to constrain state action, state governments remain partners rather than vassals in the federal system.

In Chapters 4, 5 and 6 we describe some general strategies used to reform bureaucratic agencies. We then assess these strategies by looking at their effectiveness in bringing about the desired outcomes in the reorganization of the California State Employment Service. California state officials took three important steps in their reorganization efforts: they instituted (1) new leadership; (2) new structures; and (3) new incentive systems. Our analysis of this effort shows what most students of public administration already know—that reform involves political cost and that this cost is felt not only in the political system's environment but also within the system itself. In Chapter 4 we point out an important weakness in bureaucratic reform: most high-level executive appointees have very short careers. This raises the question of how frequent changes in political leadership affect a bureaucracy, employee morale, and the goals of the reformers.

Chapter 5 suggests that different leaders use various types of structural changes in their attempts to achieve reform. The major determinants of the type used depend on the personal experience of the appointee and the stage through which the agency is passing at that time. This chapter also points out that implementation of new reforms is difficult under normal circumstances but becomes even more so when the new goals are at variance with what employees believe to be the agency's original purpose. We also stress that the question is not whether reform is possible; the real question is whether the initiators of reform have the requisite knowledge of the bureaucratic process that will be needed to alter old structures and behaviors without destroying the ability of these institutions to function in the future.

The basic theme of Chapter 6 is that people will change given proper incentives and adequate resources. Attempts by political leaders to institute reforms that deny these basic truths are likely to lead to failure, even though agency personnel themselves may wish for success. We end in Chapter 7 by looking at the implications of bureaucratic reform in a political arena characterized by a highly changing political environment with new goals and priorities. It is in such an atmosphere that a study of bureaucratic reform takes on its full meaning.

NOTES

1. State of California, Health and Welfare Agency, Employment Development Department, *Job Growth in California, 1979.* See Appendix A.

2. Richard Radda, "Reagan's Record as a State Politician," New York, *Empire State Report,* Sept. 16–30, 1980, 1–4.

The Politics of Bureaucratic Reform

Abbreviations Used in the Text

ADC	Aid to Dependent Children
AFDC	Aid to Families with Dependent Children
CAMPS	Cooperative Area Manpower Planning Systems
CEAs	Career Executive Appointment Managers
CEP	Concentrated Employment Program
CSES	California State Employment Service
DAS	Division of Apprenticeship Standards
DOL	U.S. Department of Labor
EDA	Economically Disadvantaged Area
EOA	Economic Opportunity Act
ERS	Employability Rating System
FEPC	Fair Employment Practices Commission
HEW	U.S. Department of Health, Education, and Welfare
HRD	California Human Resources Department
ICESA	Interstate Conference of Employment Security Agencies
JOBS	Job Opportunities in the Business Sector
JTDP	Job Training, Development, and Placement Division
MDTA	Manpower Development and Training Act
NAB	National Alliance of Businessmen
NYC	Neighborhood Youth Corps
OEO	Office of Economic Opportunity
OJT	On-the-Job Training
PEP	Public Employment Program
TCIP	Tax Collection and Insurance Payment Division
USES	U.S. Employment Service
WIN	Work Incentive Program

1

Models of Governmental Reform:
A Review and Critique

The 1960s were a turbulent period. During that decade the need
for solutions to many old problems as well as new ones seemed
to take on added urgency. The complexity of these problems,
along with demands by certain groups that something be done
now, brought forth an expansion of government activity—
including the reform of some old institutions and the creation
of quite a few new ones. Federal intervention into such areas as
health, education, welfare, and manpower also caused changes
in state and local practices. The aim of these government reforms was to design new delivery systems that, it was hoped,
would make institutions more responsive to the needs of the
poor, the minorities, and the unorganized.

Contrary to what is generally believed, the new delivery
systems did not focus as much on administrative problems as
they did on political ones. It was assumed that the problem of
delivery arose because administrators were unable to reach
clients, or, if they did, the relationship was unsatisfactory. That
is to say, delivery of services was seen as essentially a political
problem involving class and power rather than administrative
procedures. Based on this assumption, new systems were
designed to give political power to disadvantaged groups by
opening up the administrative process to their participation.[1]

By changing the political priorities, instituting reforms in
old agencies or creating new ones, and introducing new delivery systems, the Great Society reformers hoped to improve the

conditions of the disadvantaged. Yet by the end of the decade, most researchers and analysts regarded these programs as failures. Why?

The reasons given have been as varied as the programs themselves. Some thought the problems could be traced to rising expectations, while others believed that government was being asked to do what it could not do. Still others believed that government did not commit sufficient resources and support. Another explanation suggested that the problem was not money but knowledge about what to do with it.[2]

In the end, much of the blame was placed on the bureaucracy. Politicians and others complained that it was not the policies that were deficient; they were just poorly administered. What politicians did not concede was that the new reforms had generated a great deal of administrative disarray, which caused dysfunctions in program implementation. According to Allen Shick, these administrative deficiencies included too many categorical grant programs; overlapping planning requirements; lack of information; insufficient field authority to approve projects; overlapping regional boundaries; and unrealistic federal standards.[3] In other words, fragmentation at the national level produced dysfunction at lower levels of government.

In their comprehensive study of Great Society programs, Eli Ginzberg and Robert Solow argue that these programs were a mixture of success and failure. They suggest that the administrative goals were unrealistic because they promised everything; that lack of expertise and knowledge hampered program success; that, while Congress agreed with the goals of the administration, programs were underfunded. But they go on to suggest that the initial efforts at reform were often reasonable and cautious. Mistakes were made, but benefits also resulted.[4] The important point that these authors make is that social intervention is not always bad. Reforms can produce good results under the proper circumstances. And while the experience of the 1960s raises some significant new questions about the effectiveness of certain programs, reform is still a popular political tool.[5]

This chapter shows that the major determinants of reorganization are political. An analysis of the reasons given for reorganization and of the constraints on reorganization and a review of the current literature demonstrate that the underlying motive is political control of the power bases. The analysis also shows that understanding the success or failure of reorganization does not end with legislative enactment of new policies but also includes the process of implementing those policies in the existing bureaucratic structures.

REORGANIZATION: A NEW DEFINITION

In the folklore of public administration *reorganization* has long been associated with *reform*. Reform has a strong normative connotation. According to Webster's *Seventh Collegiate Dictionary*, reform as a noun means "change for the better"; as a verb, "change from bad to good." The term reorganization has acquired nearly the same meaning in American culture, in both its normative and descriptive senses.[6]

Reorganization as a dynamic process of the body politic has not received sufficient attention. The subject of reorganization is seldom mentioned as one of the major instruments of political power by scholars. The traditional view saw reorganization as concerning only the anatomy of organizational conflict. Indeed, the old view of reorganization was more concerned with form than with substance.

For decades Americans have been led to believe that major reorganizations involve such cherished values as economy and efficiency. In fact, the rhetoric of efficiency is a tactic used by reorganizers to divert attention from their central concerns— policy changes and the introduction of new programs. When new agencies or reforms are proposed, they are almost always presented as economy measures rather than as strategic political maneuvers. Politicians and administrators justify new programs on the basis of their potential for reducing taxes—not as the result of the private struggles of some politicians to gain control over others.

Anyone who believes that economy and efficiency are prime reasons for reorganization need only examine some of the recent reorganization proposals that have been presented to Congress. According to Harold Seidman, of the eighty-six reorganization plans transmitted to Congress between 1949 and

1969, only three were supported by precise dollar estimates of savings. The weight of empirical evidence supports President Franklin D. Roosevelt's contention that "we have to get over the notion that the purpose of reorganization is economy. The reason for reorganization is good management."[7] If this argument is true, then improving administrative management implies a desire to exercise control over decisions; in the political arena, control over decisions equals power. Reorgnaization, therefore, means removing from the control of others what the reformers want for themselves.

Historically Americans have relied upon reorganization as a tool and symbol of administrative reform. Its roots reach back into the last century. Early municipal reform efforts that advocated the strong mayor system and the commission form of government saw reorganization as a way to improve the administrative structure and to get power. Even today, the politician's solution to a complex problem is often reorganization. This is what John Gardner calls the "vending-machine" concept of social change: Put a coin in the machine, out comes a piece of candy. If there is a social problem, pass a law, and out comes a solution.[8]

In the past, then, the question was: According to the principles of management science, what is the best organization? Today, the question is: What will be the political consequences of this change on our institutions? In other words, who controls what and at whose expense?

Since most issues about reorganization today are concerned more with political questions than with questions of organizational design, we need a definition of reorganization that will permit us to understand the linkages between political processes and attempts at organizational reform in public agencies. The old principles of organization theory, with their emphasis on form, are inapplicable to current issues about reorganization. A clearer and more realistic definition is needed.

A new definition might be: *Reorganization is the continuous process through which the power and authority of an organization are redistributed in an attempt to achieve new policy outcomes.* It is also a means by which incremental change may be accelerated and legitimized throughout the organization. In this view reorganization is not accidental; it is planned change designed to achieve new policy outcomes.

Reorganization seldom involves comprehensive change. In a public bureaucracy, with an established civil service system and permanent structures, comprehensive changes are virtually impossible. It is possible, however, to make selective changes that may direct the agency toward new goals. Thus, reorganization may be understood as the selective alteration of those parts of an organization that are essential to the achievement of new goals.

Reorganization of public administrative agencies is not neutral in either intent or result. Seldom are agencies changed simply for the sake of change. The organization or reorganization of public agencies determines who will exercise power—or who will make decisions. It follows, then, that if public administrative agencies are reorganized by outsiders, the dominant forces are likely to be political. This is not to say that all reorganizations are caused by external demands. Some agencies are reorganized by the top executive, but most of these are routine reorganizations concerned more with improving management systems than with shifting authority from one group to another. As defined here, reorganization deals with the political process more than with organizational design. Major alterations of an organization's purpose and structure are normally responses to external political forces.

At every political level, the issue is: Who should allocate what, how much, and to whom? Each organizational level also reflects this struggle. Quite frequently changing an organization's structure involves the strategic and tactical uses of reorganization by political leaders and pressure groups to gain autonomy over policies and programs, using someone else's money. We contend here that conflicts between political units (e.g., federal and state governments) may cause shifts in organization structure.

Reorganization, then, is a dynamic process that moves in phases: innovation, consolidation, and reversion. Each phase of the reorganization process produces changes that lead to other changes. Thus, old policies are thawed, modified, and then refrozen. The length of each phase depends on political and economic factors.

Innovation includes not only mandated changes but also all other changes deemed necessary to the success of the enterprise. Hence, the authority to make changes is extended to policy areas other than those mandated. Changes in goals may be accompanied by changes in structure and personnel. Innovation includes the elements of incorporation, diffusion, and cooptation. Incorporation is the addition of new personnel and new structures; diffusion is the process of inculcating the new values and new goals in the members of the organization; cooptation is the attempt to bring hostile groups and old employees into the new structure through such techniques as placement on boards and into management positions. During innovation expansion is fairly extensive and allows for inclusion of diverse elements without major conflicts.

Consolidation involves an attempt to mix the most feasible elements of the old system with the best of the new. In this phase coordination becomes a desirable goal so that gains will not be lost as new modifications are made in the old structure. Consolidation usually signals an end to expansion and may be the beginning of another modification in the structure.

Reversion is characterized by attempts at integration of old and new personnel and by a return to the old structure, with symbolic assurances of protection of some of the new goals. This phase recognizes the need for organizational stability to ensure survival.

Uses of Reorganization

Reorganization is another word for shifting power and may assume a variety of forms. In the hands of an astute president it may be used to gain control of certain governmental functions at the expense of Congress. In fact, many of the reorganization attempts mentioned later in this section center on this struggle for government control between the president and Congress.

Sometimes reorganization is used to focus attention on the issue of power. A president may use reorganization to signify that control is being exerted, even if the future outcomes are uncertain, because he must do something to maintain public confidence and political confidence and support. James Carroll suggests that this may have been Jimmy Carter's motivation in his proposed reorganization of the federal Civil Service Commission.[9] In the same way reorganization may be used as a symbolic assurance that action is being or will soon be instituted. Use of reorganization as a sign of action can also be perverted to stimulate change when none is intended. Reorganizers attempt to placate the public by creating activity that is said to correct governmental abuses when no relevant change is intended. The constant reorganizations of the welfare system suggest this approach. A similar power tactic is the use of cooptation. An agency or interest group may be brought into a larger agency to diffuse their objections to a reorganization and to control their influence. In like manner agencies are physically relocated to change their receptiveness to outside influences and interest groups.

Other forms of reorganization mask the power issue. Several of these come under the category of increased effectiveness and efficiency. Reorganizations are rationalized as methods to streamline the bureaucracy. A related use of reorganization is to increase the coordination of bureaucracies. The creation of CETA (Comprehensive Employment Training Act) by President Richard Nixon was a reorganization aimed at bringing a multitude of manpower programs under a single coordinating agency. The inverse of this principle is also true: reorganization can be used to divide a single department into several smaller and often less potent agencies or to eliminate it altogether, as with Reagan's announced intention to eliminiate the Education and Energy departments. Sometimes the goals of efficiency and effectiveness are used to justify the reorganization of a new, potentially important technological innovation, e.g., atomic energy or space exploration.

A third category of reasons given for reorganization involves the improvement of administrative structure and management. The reorganization of the federal bureaucracy proposed by Carter was intended to make the executive branch more manageable. Another use of structural reorganization is for the resolution of conflicting interests by the creation of an intermediate, supervising agency. Given the complexity of the federal system, it is sometimes impossible for the president to deal with such conflicts, so he appoints an intermediary to act on his behalf; it was under such circumstances that the office of Department of Defense was created.

A final category is the use of reorganization to achieve new organizational goals, purposes, or public policy. Frederick Mosher has argued that this result is the reason why public agencies reorganize. He believes that changes in purpose cause shifts in policies and programs.[10] His argument implies that external forces sometimes determine reorganization, but he fails to recognize that the dominant external influences on public agencies are political and that most reform efforts are initiated or proposed by politicians. Policy directions are usually changed by political sources. The Model Cities concept was used to shift control from state and municipal governmental officials to community control. It was an approach used by the Lyndon Johnson administration to redistribute social programs (resources) through reorganization. In contrast, the Nixon administration used CETA to shift the control of manpower programs away from community-based organizations and to give them to local and state governments. The Reagan administration's approach includes yet another major change; categorical programs are to be taken from local governments and given to the states in the form of block grants. At other times, reorganization may ensure political survival for an agency that has lost its popular appeal or clientele by deemphasizing old goals and clientele in favor of new ones that are perceived to be politically more viable.

Reorganization is essentially a stopgap that is used when substantive issues are not amenable to easy solutions. Frequently it is used as a symbol of change or an indication that the problem will soon be solved. Quite often these symbolic assurances end up with the rhetoric going to one side and the benefits going to another. Reorganization projects the image of concern and modernity, and, thus conceived, it can be an instrument of change or an expression of intent. It is, in the final analysis, a servant and not the master. Whether it is used for worthy or unworthy purposes depends exclusively on the will of its masters.

How politicians use reorganization is one consideration, but what causes reorganization to occur is another. In the next section we briefly review the utility of three models in explaining the causes of reorganization in public agencies.

Models of Governmental Reorganization

Recognizing the many uses of reorganization and the impact it has on public administration, scholars have developed several theories to explain more fully the process and cause of governmental reorganization. A review of current literature suggests three models or perspectives that reflect these theories of reorganization: (1) reorganization as diffused innovation, (2) reorganization as adaptation to modernization, and (3) reorganization as political competition.[11] Each of these models utilizes a unique conceptual lens to explain why reorganization occurs.

Model 1: Reorganization as Diffused Innovation. This model describes a tracking system of changes passing from one governmental unit to another. Innovation is defined as "any idea, practice, or material artifact perceived to be new by the relevant unit of adoption."[12] Innovations, seen as successful by other governmental units or by researchers and consultants, are adopted intact by other governmental units. The model builds upon the concept that a new approach (innovation) can be shared by neighboring or related units. The diffusion may be passed between comparable governing units, as from one state government to another, or dissimilar ones, as from the federal government to a state government. The diffusion of the innovation may occur in several ways. It may be the result of sharing information about common problems, or it may occur when consultants from one research firm assist in designing reorganization plans for several governmental units. Similarly, one government may decide to emulate a change it sees in another unit. For example, the Hoover Commission, an innovative approach to dealing with federal reorganization, spread throughout the nation as many states designated commissions to study state reorganization. Those state commissions were referred to as "little Hoover Commissions," indicative of their imitation of the federal approach. The development of a manpower service for the disadvantaged in California, the illustration used in this book, was precisely this sort of imitated innovation. Innovation/diffusion as a model is helpful in tracking innovations in forms of governmental reorganization throughout the United States and explains why similar systems may be found in Maine and Mississippi. It also clarifies the role of persons and agencies in boundary-spanning positions who function as agents of diffusion.

While this model tracks a pattern of reorganization in diverse units, it does not explain the origin of the innovation. It does not explain the how, where, or who of an innovation, nor does it help other reformers discover how to start their own reorganizations. Also the model does not effectively filter out other relevant, explanatory variables. For example, two states—such as Arkansas and Alabama—with comparable populations, fiscal problems, and social concerns may adopt similar policies at the same time. Is diffusion the main causal force in this duplication, or are the basic similarities in conditions and circumstances in the two states such that the reorganizations were a natural response to their environments? Finally, the use of this model is dysfunctional in that it does not encourage reformers to individualize their reorganization designs to fit their unique governmental units. In fact, the attempt to transfer an innovation that is successful in one system to another system frequently ends in failure.

Model 2: Reorganization as Adaptation to Modernization. This model deals with reorganization at the macro level, i.e., it uses an entire society as its unit of analysis. It suggests that as the environment changes it produces different demands on organizational structures. Organizations must then modify their structures or goals to be more responsive to the larger environment. In this model the organization is not the creator of change, but the adapter to change that has already occurred.

A leading proponent of this view is Herbert Kaufman.[13] Basing his analysis on the American social structure, he identified three core values that he feels had a significant impact on the form of government used in this country: representativeness, neutral competence, and executive leadership. Some combination of these values is always present within the total value structure of the United States, but each has enjoyed a period of dominance in American history. The first of these values, representativeness, was prominent from the Revolutionary War until after the Jacksonian period. During this time Americans were anxious to assure representativeness (that each government official gained power only through election and that that power was revokable through election). In the early 1800s it became apparent that abuses had developed from this overattachment to representativeness. One of the most obvious abuses was the excessively long election ballot. Government critics began to campaign for a system based on neutral competence, where government agency heads obtained jobs based on their skills and competence and not on political patronage. The value stressed separating the performance of government functions from the political process. Later, problems inherent in this approach also surfaced. Experts, while competent at their individual jobs, were not able to coordinate overall governmental activity. This lack of coordination in services encouraged the movement to the third core value—executive leadership. A strong leader was sought to direct and coordinate the activities of the government and to promote the "public good." With each of these core values change was promoted by the larger social forces contained in the environment.

This model serves to explain environmental conditions needed for change. It helps to explain why, for example, CETA legislation was passed in 1973—during a period of growing unemployment—and not earlier, although similar legislation had been proposed. While this model is helpful in understanding the circumstances that are conducive to change, it does not predict when change will happen. The appropriate conditions do not always produce the anticipated change. This inability to identify when change will occur leaves the reorganizer without tools to improve his or her reorganization attempts.

Model 3: Reorganization as Political Competition. The third model differs from the other two because it deals with the process as well as the cause of reorganization. It defines reorganization as part of the larger political process that produces a political outcome or product. The decisionmakers in this model are concerned with power: to gain power, to retain power, to rearrange power, or to secure a power base. The key element of the model is the competition between different political groups to gain control of the power base. These elements are also found in the definition of reorganization presented earlier: *the process through which the power and authority of an organization are redistributed in an attempt to achieve new policy outcomes.* According to this model, policy choices such as reorganization are based on the control of power, and the greatest political benefits often take priority over the greatest public benefits. The justification for a reorganization is often based on its political end rather than its policy product. The concept of rational decisionmaking is replaced with the best political choice.

The conceptual model of reorganization as a political process increases the organizer's understanding of how major an influence political considerations are in the reorganization process. The objectives of reorganization, as well as its products, are political. The validity of this view can be seen in the processes involved in several major federal reorganization plans since 1930: "the efforts toward federal executive reorganization since 1932 may be interpreted as an alliance between the chief executive and a rising group of professional administrators to strengthen the presidential position and conversely weaken the absolute veto power of the congressional committees and group pressure over proposals for organization of federal agencies."[14]

FDR was one of the first presidents to advocate federal reorganization. As an astute politician, he was aware that new organizational structures could be used to deny access to others. As a capable administrator, he was also aware that control of the federal bureaucracy was essential to the implementation of his New Deal programs. He also knew that to gain needed management control of the bureaucracy he would have to take control away from Congress and lodge it in the executive branch. He thus sought from Congress permission to reorganize the federal structure. The reorganization proposals of 1937–39 were defeated by Congress. Accounts of that period indicate congressional concern that Roosevelt's reorganization attempts would make him a mini-director. In other words, it was congressional fear of a shift in power from Congress to the president, not the design of the reorganization, that brought about the defeat of these attempts. The defeats would have been considered irrational if the executive branch and FDR had viewed them as part of anything other than the political process. That reorganization plans were passed in 1939 and 1945 in the "face of such attitudes and considerations can truly be regarded as a major feat of political strategy."[15]

Another restructuring move of FDR's involved the Supreme Court. The court had become a major obstacle to New Deal programs—rejecting many of them as unconstitutional. To change that power base, FDR proposed reorganizing the court by expanding the number of judges on the bench. He sought this move to gain greater presidential support from the court. He failed, but the case illustrates how politicians may attempt to use reorganization as a tool to increase their influence or to threaten those who disagree with them.

Variations on this pattern of reorganizing the federal structure have been used by every president. During the Nixon years, the power base sought was political support in local and state governments. Nixon's strategy was to reward these supporters by channeling federal funds to their governmental units through revenue-sharing and thereby maintain their political support. Such reorganization was called "decentralizing" the federal bureaucracy, and the political plum was the local discretionary use of funds rather than the customary federal dictation.

President Carter also sought to reorganize the federal structure. Like his predecessors, Carter recognized that the federal bureaucracy was out of the control of the executive branch. In fact, some political observers, such as Jack Anderson, have written that "the death rattle resounding across the land is the result of a disease called 'bureaucracy.' "[16] One of Carter's approaches to this problem was to reorganize the federal civil service. Carter's proposals sought to "change the current organization of power, increasing the power of the presidency and political management at the expense of bureaucrats, parties, unions, interest groups, and parts of Congress."[17]

The sources of power that Carter contended with included both the bureaucracy and Congress. Carter had to offer the bureaucracy sufficient incentives to entice them to let go of some of their power. The proposed Senior Executive Service (SES) may demonstrate this point. Carter could not force the bureaucrats into the program because of their civil service protection and job tenure. In order to get volunteers, incentives of extra money and higher job status were offered, with—it should be added—surprising success.

President Reagan, on the other hand, has used budgetary reductions to change programmatic and policy directions. The administration is also using the block grant as a way to reduce the budget and shift power from Washington to the states. Reagan's approach to block grants differs from that used by Nixon-Ford in that all block grants involve significant cuts in spending; the payment of federal grants are to states only— another shift in political direction.

The model of reorganization as political competition offers the student of reorganization an increased appreciation of the role of politics in the process. This perspective also increases the political realities of the reorganization process and outcome. However, the model has some disadvantages. Its view of reorganization can become pessimistic when too much emphasis is placed on political goals at the expense of the public good. It also has not fared any better than the other two models when it comes to testing.

Constraints on Reorganization

Reorganizations are often reflective of or shaped by environmental constraints, some of which may be described as follows: (1) a conservative, anti-reorganization attitude from the legislature, reflecting concern about placing more power in the executive branch; (2) the resistance to change of bureaucratic structures; (3) the political cost of failure to the reorganizers, the party in power; (4) inadequate information about reorganizational goals or purposes. This lack of knowledge may run the gamut from reorganization for inappropriate reasons to bureaucrats failing to implement the change in the desired form; (5) mixed, contradictory messages about reorganization goals when the political process leaves goals unclear, on purpose, to assure legislative enactment. The dilemma is then passed on to the bureaucracy, which lacks the tools to deal with the problem;

(6) limited resources; and (7) the resistance of the public and of client groups.

Frequently the constraints or the opposition to reorganization reflects the process of political competition more than the goals and plans of reorganizers. For instance, the location of employment and unemployment services within the Department of Labor (DOL) was strongly opposed by both state employment agencies and employers. This opposition was based on a fear of federalization of the employment system. Under FDR and Reorganization Plan 1, the function of unemployment compensation was moved out of DOL. In 1944 it was returned to DOL not only at its request but also to relieve some of the difficulties arising from the war effort. The employment service employees had already been moved out of state control and into the federal system in response to war-time employment problems. At the end of the war, the powerful coalition of state employment agencies and employers succeeded in returning this function to the states.

In 1949—in Reorganization Plan 2—President Harry Truman suggested that the unemployment compensation and employment services again be combined under DOL. The department had lobbied for this move because it believed the provision of these services was vital to its own survival. The Hoover Commission had also recommended this move because it assessed DOL as administratively weak and in need of a more viable function. Opposition to this plan immediately surfaced from a coalition of state agencies and employers, which had just regained control of the employment services. The state agencies feared federal control and disliked having the form of employment services dictated to them. Employers were likewise concerned about more federal control and increased financial costs. Under the system at that time employers were taxed at the rate of 3 percent to pay for employment services. This tax was usually reduced at the discretion of individual states in response to "good employment practices." Neither group wanted the federal government involved in that process. It is obvious that this opposition was not in response to the consolidation of two related services under one administrative agency; rather it was in response to a change in authority and power.

The movement to reform the California manpower service in the 1960s, which is detailed later in this book, demonstrates the role of political competition and process in such a change. Key political forces—then Governor Reagan and his office, former Speaker Jesse Unruh and the Democratically controlled legislature, and the federal government—were in conflict with each other over control of employment services in California. State politicians saw the new federal emphasis on the disadvantaged as an opportune time to wrest some of the political power away from the federal system. The competition that this move created helped to dictate the form of the new program and also the form of its failures.

POLITICAL PROCESS MODEL: AN ALTERNATIVE VIEW

Each of the models discussed above seems to center on one aspect of the reorganization process and to neglect other relevant features. The model of diffused innovation provides an effective tracking system on reorganization but fails to explain how innovations are developed initially. The model of reorganization as adaptation to modernization details the impact of environmental conditions on reorganization. While favorable environmental conditions are a necessary feature of reorganization, they are not sufficient to assure success or implementation of the reorganization design. The model of political competition clarifies the importance of the political role in the final outcome but fails to show the relationship between the process and its final outcome.

Since none of these models separately seems to deal with the issue of governmental reorganization in totality, perhaps synthesizing them will. To gain a clearer understanding of how these models of reorganization might be blended together, we developed a flowchart detailing some of the factors involved in the manpower situation in California (Figure 1).

But even this combined model has a missing element. What is not explained is the form of the final product. What sorts of changes can take place in the reorganization policy between the

Figure 1
A Synthesis of Models of Reorganization

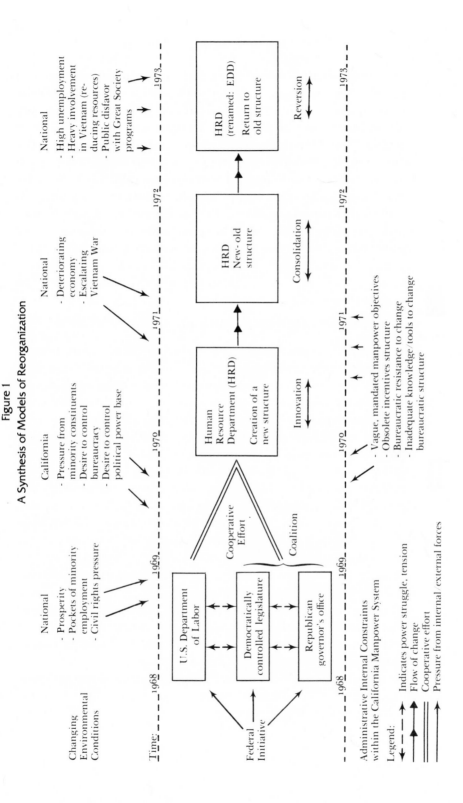

time it is designed and enacted and the time it becomes part of the bureaucracy? One of the aims of this book is to take the initial reorganization of the California State Employment Service as it was legislatively enacted, to follow it through to its conclusion, and then to evaluate its final product. It becomes apparent that there is a longer process involved in reorganization than the legislative acceptance of it. Paul Berman, in "The Study of Macro- and Micro-Implementation," suggests that the rest of this process is the implementation of the reorganization plan and policy choices.[18] As mentioned earlier, implementation is a process that seeks to "carry out an authoritative decision." Jeffrey L. Pressman and Aaron Wildavsky, as cited by Berman, have suggested "that a policy decision, a plan to reorganize, implies a theory which relates goals to expected ends or consequences: this theory assumes that once a policy choice, P, is made then outcome, O, will occur." Implementation analysis states that the theory is not correct: that events—variables—affect the policy choice, P, and prevent its reaching outcome, O. Berman suggests that one such major variable is the interaction of the policy with the institutional setting. This case study will explore the interaction between the policy decision, which stated that the employment service should change its goals from servicing the job-ready and the employer to servicing the disadvantaged and the hard core unemployed, and the institutional setting of the California State Employment Service during this period.

The study of the California manpower system will question some of the assumptions of the models of reorganization. The questions do not involve the structure of the models as such but rather the failure of these models to capture and evaluate the final product of the reorganization. The issue is not whether reorganization occurred, but how successfully the reorganization plan was implemented or institutionalized within the organizational structure. Also an attempt is made to identify where the failure rests when the final product does not take the form the policymakers desire. One question to be asked in Chapter 2 is whether the blame properly belongs with the bureaucracy, where it is so often placed. Does not failure perhaps also rest with the policymakers who failed to consider the implementation process, the appropriateness of their design, and the effect of the policy on the institutional setting?

This study also explores other relevant variables within the reorganization process. What power do local agencies have in determining how reorganization policy decisions are implemented? How important is the institutionalization of the new structure? Berman suggests that an implemented practice may be short-lived unless officials take appropriate actions to institutionalize it, i.e., to make implemented practices part of standard operating procedure.[19] In the same article Donald Schon is quoted as saying, "But stable organizations have a knack of allowing new and even 'successful' practice to fade away, especially when the macro-policy that precipitated local adoption is no longer an idea in good currency."[20] An investigation of the political and administrative reform of the California State Employment Service should begin to integrate the process of policy decisionmaking with the implementation process and its intended consequences. An exploration of the partial failure of the change in California should help pinpoint the junctures at which the political decisions and activities of the participants dictated the final political outcome.

NOTES

1. Allen Schick, "The Trauma of Politics" (paper prepared for the annual conference of the National Association of Schools of Public Affairs and Administration, Syracuse, N.Y., May 2–5, 1976).

2. Ibid., 8–9.

3. Ibid., 10.

4. Ginzberg and Solow, *The Great Society: Lessons for the Future* (New York: Basic Books, 1974), 211–20.

5. "Big Government in Carter Plan," Champaign-Urbana *News-Gazette,* June 11, 1976.

6. Frederick Mosher, "Some Notes on the Reorganization of Public Agencies," in *Public Administration and Democracy: Essays in Honor of Paul H. Appleby,* ed. Roscoe C. Martin (Syracuse, N.Y.: Syracuse University Press, 1965), 130.

7. Seidman, *Politics, Position and Power: The Dynamics of Federal Organization* (New York: Oxford University Press, 1970), 12.

8. As quoted in ibid., 65.

9. James Carroll, "Up the Bureaucracy: Reorganization and Reforming the Federal Civil Service" (paper presented at the national conference of the American Society for Public Administration, Phoenix, Ariz., 1978, 10–11).

10. Mosher, ed., *Governmental Reorganization: Cases and Commentaries* (New York: Bobbs-Merrill Co., 1967), 494–96.

11. These models reflect the synthesis of the literature as found in James L. Garnett and Charles H. Levine, "State Executive Branch Reorganization: Perspectives, Patterns, and Action Guides" (paper delivered at the annual meeting of the Midwest Political Science Association, Chicago, Ill., Apr. 1978).

12. Gerald Zaltman, Robert Duncan, and Johnny Holbek, *Innovations and Organizations* (New York: John Wiley & Sons, 1973).

13. Kaufman, "Emerging Conflict in the Doctrines of Public Administration," *American Political Science Review*, 50 (Dec. 1956), 1057–73.

14. Avery Leiserson, "Political Limitations on Executive Reorganization," ibid., 41 (Mar. 1953), 69–70.

15. Ibid., 72.

16. Carroll, "Up the Bureaucracy," 1.

17. Ibid., 2.

18. Berman, "The Study of Macro- and Micro-Implementation," *Public Policy*, 26, (Spring 1978), 160.

19. Ibid., 177.

20. Ibid., 178.

2

Bureaucratic Reform and Public Policy

People wonder why certain programs fail. The normal tendency is to blame failure on the bureaucracy.[1] "Slow moving," "unresponsive," and "disloyal" are among the mildest words used to describe bureaucracies. If programs are to be successful in this view, bureaucracy must be made more responsive; activities need to be reorganized and the bureaucrats recirculated to prevent stagnation. Bureaucrats are also criticized for their inability to provide dramatic and imaginative proposals to the legislature. Seldom are politicians criticized for the failure of a program; the fault is normally attributed to incompetent and stupid administrators.

How did bureaucrats get such a negative image? Is it deserved? If it is, what are the causes? We argue here that while it is true that most bureaucrats resist change out of a desire to protect their own self-interest,[2] their behavior is actually determined by two flaws in the American policymaking process: (1) the inability of policymakers to make clear choices between incompatible but valued alternatives, and (2) policymakers' tendency to use an existing instrument regardless of how well its present product fits the new needs. In short, a large part of bureaucratic behavior is a by-product of the ambiguity that exists in the national political arena where policymaking takes place.

Given the ambiguity and flaws at the national level, public organizations can seldom be counted on to achieve all of the outcomes desired by public officials. This is because public organizations evolve from the political process; their purposes and structure are normally the result of political compromises. People take what they can get rather than waiting for the perfect instrument. In addition, the structure of an organization is a product of its initiators. Thus, for example, an organization built on the model of personnel management in the late 1920s and 1930s may well be ill-suited to carry out new purposes in the 1960s. The flaws in the policy process, then, are likely to produce both internal and systemic obstacles to the effective implementation of public policy.[3]

INCOMPATIBLE POLICY CHOICES

The first flaw in the policymaking process in the United States is the inability of policymakers to make clear choices between incompatible but valued alternatives. How this flaw can lead to internal resistance to change is illustrated in a series of events involving the California Employment Service.

The Federal-State Employment Service (or U.S. Employment Service [USES]) was established as a result of the Wagner-Peyser Act of 1933, which was passed as a direct response to the joblessness caused by the economic depression of the 1930s. It mandated the creation of a national system of employment offices to be administered by a new division of the Department of Labor (DOL).[4]

USES began as an attempt to rationalize the labor market by reducing unemployment to an acceptable minimum and by providing better information between work seekers and employers. During its early history the employment service was in competition with private agencies and the personnel units of private firms. This led to screening the potential labor pool in behalf of employers. The emphasis of the employment service during this time was on the accurate identification of individual qualifications and of job requirements, so that open positions would be filled and unnecessary unemployment avoided. (The development of the occupational classification dictionary by the USES research section is an indication of the technical view the agency took of its task.) Almost from the very outset the employment service was forced to take responsibility for the work test required by the unemployment compensation system. Employees were required to register with the USES for a job before they could apply for and receive unemployment compensation. This link between unemployment compensation and USES was the beginning of a series of unwanted relationships.

The high point of the employment service's existence came during World War II, when it was federalized and returned to DOL (from which it had been separated in 1939 and given to the Social Security Board). After the war the agency was returned to the states and was put back into an uncomfortable relationship with unemployment compensation. The USES people continued to be preoccupied with employer relations, while the unemployment compensation people were primarily concerned with efficient administration of the unemployment insurance system. Employment service personnel concentrated on "penetrating" the job market as far as possible: the measure of their success was the percentage of all known hirings arranged by the service.

Although the Wagner-Peyser Act states that the employment service is to serve all applicants "legally qualified to engage in employment,"[5] the practice was to send out only highly qualified workers. This pattern of service to the employer developed as a result of the frequent periods of economic downturn (a labor surplus and a low demand for labor) during the 1930s and after World War II. The need to entice employers to utilize its services became the prime focus of much of state employment service's efforts: "Local office staffs tended to refer only the best qualified applicants to fill job orders in the hope that employers would thus be encouraged to send in more job orders.... In time, this became the accepted practice."[6]

Another pattern that developed in the 1930s and 1940s that influenced state employment service operations was the funding arrangement. At first the federal government put up half the money from the general fund and required the states to supply the other half. In 1935 the Social Security Act was passed, joining employment service and unemployment insurance and providing a more stable funding source. As a result of these funding arrangements, state offices were under tight federal control, and the control became even tighter after a 1949 amendment to the Wagner-Peyser Act that eliminated the matching provisions.

After 1949 the employment service operations were paid for from the federal unemployment insurance tax on employers, giving this group a special, if not privileged, interest in employment service administration.[7] The link between unemployment compensation and the employers acted to deflect the original mission of the service.

Thus, as a federally imposed responsibility, the employment service became the instrument for varying but ever-expanding efforts to increase employment opportunities for various groups of disadvantaged people, including women in the Aid to Dependent Children (ADC) and Aid to Families with Dependent Children (AFDC) programs. Clearly this effort went against the long-held purpose of maximizing the service's role in all employment transactions and of providing the most complete pool of job opportunities and available applicant information possible. These new responsibilities did not agree with the agency's service philosophy and self-image; the agency also suffered constant threats (discussed later in this chapter) because of the requirements that it handle tasks inimical to its self-image and philosophy. Budgeting by work units did not help, since budgets were held to a very narrowly defined work load and to unit-cost measurement procedures.[8]

The unwanted relationship with unemployment compensation (the requirement that the applicants register for employment) had parallels to the later relation of USES to new manpower priorities: the work test was a *coercive,* not a *cooperative,* relationship for clients; later efforts to promote minority employment had potential and implicit coercive aspects in relations with employers.

The history of the employment service, then, reflects a constant characteristic of policymaking in the United States—the substitution of apparently technical criteria for making policy choices between incompatible but valued alternatives. Indeed, the entire Social Security Act, in which employment security was embedded, settled for what was legislatively possible. And although the people asked to assist in developing USES had radically different views of what was desirable and possible, the recommended legislation neither reconciled views nor adopted one analytically consistent alternative over another. The result was that the efforts of the employment service to assist the jobless were organized and supported in such a way that it could work with only the best organized and most articulate employers and employees who most nearly fitted the highly specific job qualifications these employers were encouraged to present. Moreover, the service was asked to administer a work test by referring as many compensation recipients as possible, regardless of their suitability for the available openings. USES did not regard the increase in total unemployment or the need to assist those not presently in the labor market (nor acceptable to it) as part of its responsibility. Like many other government agencies, the employment service developed a unique outlook reflecting its own customs, traditions, and history.[9] In time, these internal norms and processes became serious obstacles to agency reform.

Internal Obstacles

Sometimes people are asked to do things that they do not know how to do; or they are given contradictory demands that leave them confused; or they are asked to carry out tasks without the necessary resources. According to Herbert Kaufman, internal resistance to change is based on several factors.:[10] (1) Members of organizations seek regularity or repetitive behavior, since collective wisdom favors the status quo; while what exists may be wrong, what is unknown may be worse. (2) An individual or an entire group may seek to protect a prevailing advantage; some resist even though they know they will not be injured in order to gain concessions from new groups, while others resist because of psychic cost—they fear possible demotion. (3) Shifts in status are often responsible for the introduction of new techniques and new purposes. (4) Change involves risk and the possibility of failure.[11] (5) Programmed behavior sometimes produces conformity while limiting discretion. For this reason, in many agencies the manual of rules becomes the bible from which all wisdom and authority flows.

Some other reasons for bureaucratic resistance are the prescribed limits on bureaucratic authority and responsibility, the division of work, and the concern with accountability. Given these factors, lawfulness may not encourage the exercise of discretion (as in police work). And as bureaucrats become consumed with the day-to-day problems of the organization, they may develop tunnel vision. Their insulation from the outside world reinforces inflexibility.[12]

The by-product of all this, according to Kaufman, is that bureaucrats are not only disturbed but also astounded when change is proposed. They come to believe that what they are doing is right; if adjustments are needed, they should be made in small increments.[13] Thus, those who propose radical changes are seen as enemies of the agency. The bureaucrats' disposition is to assimilate proposals for change to established norms and procedures. We shall illustrate some of these points by showing how the old norms worked to the advantage of some clients and to the disadvantages of others.

Theoretically, bureaucrats are supposed to approach the public impartially and impersonally. The same rules and objective criteria are used for all clients. Supposedly the same policy would apply to black as well as white clients. But with racial bias so deep-seated and pervasive in American society, can bureaucrats be expected to approach the public in "a spirit of formalistic impersonality, 'sine ira et studio,' without hatred or passion, and hence without affection or enthusiasm?"[14]

The old employment service (referred to here as old in contrast to the reorganized structure) was not responsive to minorities. The employment service was a replica of the societal values that existed at the time of its creation. The general practice was to know employers' wants and needs and to refer only qualified people to them for possible employment. Before the 1960s minorities were not classified as the "most qualified" applicants by most employers.

In his initial study of the employment service, Peter Blau maintained that little discrimination existed because the greater the influence of production on officials, the less their operating decisions were subject to bias. He later stated, "A neutral instrument does not actively correct existing inequalities but perpetuates them, and this is what the previous interpretation overlooked. . . . Often, however, the discrimination practices of white officials have their roots not in their own bias against Negroes but in the discriminatory demands made by the powerful employers who make hiring decisions. In these cases, a bureaucratic institution that makes officials more of a neutral instrument will by no means attenuate their discriminatory practices; only a change in power conditions will do so."[15] As Blau's statement indicates, human activity is seldom unbiased. Although the employment service was looked upon as a neutral instrument, in actuality it served the needs of employers more than those of the applicants. Applicants were screened in or screened out based on job orders from employers. The procedures and standards used for screening and testing applicants effectively excluded minorities.

The California State Employment Service (CSES) was one of the first state agencies that attempted to end past discrimination policies. Shortly after the state had established the California Fair Employment Practices Commission (FEPC) in about 1961, the director of the CSES sent out a memo stating that the agency was not to accept discriminatory orders from employers. While most officials agree that this order stopped the most blatant kinds of discrimination, it did not stop certain interviewers from continuing their old practices. Minorities found that they were still not welcome in the CSES offices. If they applied, they might return three or four times without getting a job or a referral. A placement interviewer of the CSES put it this way: "The applicant could come back if he wanted to, but that was up to him; the agency assumed no responsibility for his problem. If they didn't have a job that they could match him with, that was *his* problem."

In 1963 the DOL received reports of continued widespread discrimination in the employment service against minority groups—discrimination in referring applicants and in the hiring practices of the agency itself. In order to remedy this defect, DOL allocated to each state office a number of new positions designed to help improve service to qualified minority applicants—minority specialists.

The clientele the minority specialist ended up with seldom resembled the program description. As one minority specialist put it, "In the first place, if a minority person or anybody else hit the office who had readily marketable skills, he didn't need to see the minority specialist to get a job. He'd just come in and fill out an application and when the receptionist took a look at his experience, he'd go to the appropriate officers who'd refer him out and get a placement. The minority specialist didn't even see those people with skills, so what he really wound up with was the guy with the marginal skills that other people couldn't place and he couldn't either." In short, the minority specialist became a miracle worker without a magic wand. The job agent was to become his counterpart in the new system.

Aside from minority specialists, the old CSES had few minority employees. Few minorities were to be found at either the supervisory or managerial levels of the CSES prior to 1967. Those who were in the agency were either at the Employment Security Office I or II level or on the custodial staff. In describing minority hiring before 1967, one official said, "We didn't have minorities in any . . . I can't say any, but we had damn few minorities involved in the management level—pretty much white and male across the top. The number two man in the department was Chinese, and he had been around a hundred years, and there was one black man in Sacramento who was probably second or third level, but you know, that was about all the visibility we had. We had a couple of Chicano guys who were district supervisors and a few Chicano managers—I don't know if we had any black managers at all."

A System of Rules: Real and Implied. A placement interviewer in 1961, taking an order from an employer with whom he had previously worked, remembered what the personnel officer had said over the phone: "You know what kind of people to send, right?" The employer asked for a well-groomed receptionist with typing skills. In searching his files the interview stopped on the application card of a qualified person, but by the address, the name, his memory, or the unofficial code mark on the application card, the interviewer was aware that the applicant was black. He had only to flick his finger and go to the next card to find an equally qualified white applicant. To do this did not require an inordinate degree of racial prejudice. One respondent put it this way, "It required only an awareness of the incentive. To stop his finger and refer the black applicant required a heroic commitment to racial equality. The possible rewards that went with the white applicant were a placement count, a satisfied employer who would call again. The possible punishment for referring the black applicant was precious time spent with no statistical count, an angry employer, no more orders, and, despite the official agency policy against discrimination, something less than a gold star from supervisors and fellow employees."[16]

Another view of the structural impediments to change may be best illustrated by the following comment:

Imagine a completion interviewer handling an application card so poorly completed by the applicant that the interviewer runs well over his allotted twelve minutes to pull together a coherent work history. He patiently reworks the application card so that it is fit for office records and the critical eye of the supervisor. But the interviewer, already nervous from the baleful glances of both the supervisor and those waiting, is hardly going to take the time to teach the applicant how to fill out a decent application for work so that when he applies for a job at a company personnel office, he might stand a chance of getting it. After all, the next applicant might be a skilled secretary—a sure placement.[17]

For even the most skeptical, it does not take much to see that the entire system militated against the hard-to-place—who were largely the poor, the black, and the disadvantaged—despite the services for special groups of applicants. The system was structured in such a way that the need was to scan the supply, find those who needed the least help, and place them as quickly as possible. Thus the formal rules of the organization, plus external pressure from employers, acted as constraints to internal change.

It is assumed, as Max Weber states, that "all operations are governed by a consistent system of abstract rules [and] consist in the application of these rules to a particular case."[18] This bureaucratic process was adhered to almost without deviation in the employment service. For each function there was a line manual, reflecting state and national policy and providing exact and precise instructions. The scope of the interviewer's job as well as that of every other position was frozen into the manual. There were separate manuals for completion, order-taking, referral, selection, counseling, clerical, and supervisory positions. A manual also existed for each of the special applicant groups, such as the handicapped and veterans. Almost all conceivable possibilities were provided for. If conditions changed, amendments were added. It did not take long for a new employee to recognize the importance of the manual.

The goal of the supervisor was to ensure that the staff did precisely and exactly what the manual prescribed as quickly as possible. The ideal was a smooth, well-ordered operation. Most supervisory effort and time went into concerns with minor infractions—three-minute tardiness, extra time for coffee breaks, didn't sign in, or didn't sign out. The emphasis was on efficiency; standardized rules were devised to maintain conformity and keep the operation running as smoothly as possible without conflicts.

Innovations, shortcuts, new ideas, and questions concerning the validity of any function were neither invited nor encouraged. Employees who did make adjustments were careful not to be caught, lest they be looked upon as troublemakers. One official in the old CSES stated, "People were very conscious of the manual and the manual requirements. I think some people were overly conscious, not being aware that the manual was a guideline and permitted a great deal of latitude and flexibility. I never felt bound by the thing. I thought that it was a helpful tool. And it was always a shock to some people that the manual says for those cases that don't fit, use your own discretion. Most people didn't."

Organizations apply formal rules to simplify decisionmaking and to ensure that clients get equal treatment. By making the conditions sufficiently favorable or the penalities sufficiently desirable, organizations try to make certain that the rules are carried out in the manner intended.[19] Yet rules have powerful unintended consequences. For example, agency personnel develop professional values that in time become deeply ingrained in the institutional fabric. When rules and professional norms are congruent, agency goals are carried forward. When the norms of professionalism conflict with the norms of the agency, however, the achievement of organizational goals is hampered,

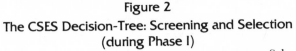

Figure 2
The CSES Decision-Tree: Screening and Selection
(during Phase I)

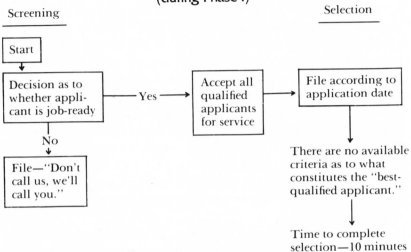

especially when professional values are reinforced by those of similar professional groups. In the employment service professional norms saw to it that those who needed the most were helped the least.

Because of the large labor surplus and low labor demand in the 1930s and after World War II, agency personnel saw employers as their chief constituency. Applicants were screened, tested, and counseled to make sure they met the exact needs of employers. When they did not, they were not referred. Figure 2 illustrates the screening and selection functions of the agency.

The decision rules in Figure 3 illustrate how the supposedly neutral rules of the employment service ended up helping some and not others. In times of low labor demand even qualified applicants are not likely to receive good service. In times of high labor demand the applicant on file will receive services, but the walk-in, job-ready applicant is more likely to receive better service than others equally qualified.[20] Figure 3 shows the winners and losers according to the norms established by the employment service.

The norm of the employment service staff was placing the

Figure 3
Employment Service: Who Wins? Who Loses?

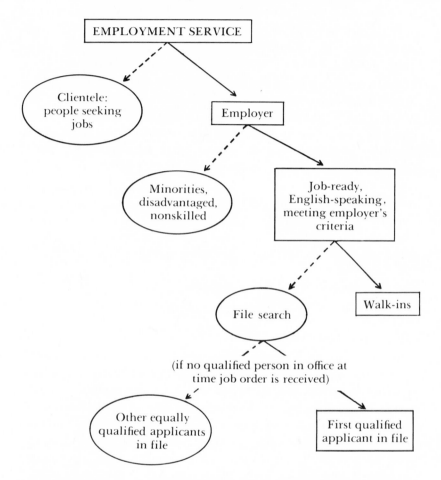

The person who is served is the job-ready applicant who is in the office at the time the job order is received. If no job-ready applicant is in the office at the time, then the first qualified applicant in the file is served.

———————→ Accept   (In terms of this diagram, accept means
                            to be given priority service;
- - - - - - - → Reject   reject means not receiving this
                            priority service or receiving little
                            if any service from the agency.)

largest amount of people in the least amount of time for a given amount of money. Lacking funds to serve all, the employment service decided the most efficient use of resources would be to serve those who could be placed the fastest with the expenditure of the least amount of resources. However, under certain circumstances efficient action may lead to undesirable consequences. Applied by the CSES, for instance, the criterion of lowest cost per person would lead to employment almost entirely of the job-ready rather than the non-job-ready. With this norm, CSES officials could remain confident that they were making professional decisions. They could look back at the number of placements made, the ratio of placements to referrals, and the number of job orders filled. Questions raised by the fact that some people were not employed could be rationalized by asserting that those that want service will seek to develop the requisite skills and attitudes desired by employers. This assumption perpetuated the status quo—the "winners" continued to win and the "losers" continued to lose.

SYSTEM OVERLOAD

The second major flaw in policymaking in the United States is the tendency to take an existing instrument and use it regardless of the similarities or dissimilarities between its present product and the new uses to which it is put. An existing instrument (the employment service) was used to provide unemployment insurance (developed under the Social Security Act) to unemployed applicants. Subsequently the service was asked to perform a whole series of actions inconsistent or only partly consistent with its original design.

While organizational adaptation is certainly desirable in a bureaucratic organization, it is also logical that one of the basic requirements of effective public policymaking is to find instruments suitable to a purpose and to see clearly the relationship between instrument and purpose. But where new programs are grafted onto old structures without a proper assessment of the relationship between the existing instrument and the new purpose, the results are likely to lead to faulty implementation of new programs and a failure of organizational reform. The fault here is probably with the policymakers rather than with the bureaucrats.

One example might suffice: USES was built according to the rationale of personnel management of the late 1920s and 1930s and staffed at the top by people who had helped develop that rationale. The federal requirement for administration and the later budgetary practices linked to full federal funding carried the original notion to its ultimate dysfunctional conclusion. Some of these dysfunctional consequences may become clearer through an examination of the impacts that the manpower legislation passed between 1960 and 1968 had on the employment service.

In the 1960s the plight of the nation's disadvantaged citizens became the focus of national attention. As noted earlier in this chapter, reports reaching DOL showed evidence of widespread discrimination in the treatment of minority and disadvantaged citizens. These reports also indicated that existing governmental programs were ill-suited to deal with the problems of the disadvantaged, the hard-core unemployed, and the minorities, who were most in need of help. The reports also suggested that something had to be done to bring these people into the mainstream of American life. Legislative and presidential leadership ultimately succeeded in obtaining laws aimed at improving national policy on employment and income redistribution.

As a result of shifts at the national level, CSES became involved in a number of efforts to increase employment for the disadvantaged. These efforts concentrated on skills development and training and to some extent discipline and motivation. To a more limited extent the service also sought to restructure jobs and create new job opportunities for the less experienced and the less highly qualified. To carry out these tasks, the employment service primarily used its existing operations and competencies: locating, testing, and screening applicants for training and work experience, attempting to place graduates, and trying to open up job opportunities for new categories of candidates.

During this period, USES was faced with a serious threat to

its survival. Organizationally, the greatest threat to its resources and jurisdiction was the Office of Economic Opportunity (OEO), since most other efforts were limited and ad hoc
(like the Work Incentive Program) or handled through friendly
contracting agencies (like federal manpower administration
and vocational education staffs). OEO also had the capacity
and authority to set up trainee selection programs, to develop
training contracts providing subsidized job opportunities, and
to handle placements. All of this it did through indigenous
personnel hired without respect to normal governmental personnel procedures.

The new task of USES was to divide resources between ongoing commitments and the provision of staff facilities for those
parts of the operation entrusted to it by administrators of several programs; it had to negotiate with uncontrolled agencies
(like OEO) for whatever parts of programs it could get. Not to
succeed was to risk obsolescence; to succeed was to absorb some
rather indigestible activities and perhaps people. Thus, the
new manpower legislation added additional burdens to the
traditional employment service.

Manpower legislation and programs from 1960 to 1968 developed from three major acts: the Manpower Development and
Training Act (MDTA) of 1962 as amended in 1963, 1966, and
1968; the Economic Opportunity Act (EOA) of 1964; and the
Social Security Act of 1967, known as the Work Incentive
Program (WIP). These acts provided a multiplicity of programs designed to serve a varied clientele, most of whom were
disadvantaged.

In 1960 the total funds appropriated by Congress for various
manpower programs, including grants to states for the Federal-
State Employment Service, approximated $300 million. By
1968 this sum had increased to $2.2 billion, and in 1972 it
reached approximately $4.2 billion.[21] The funding agencies
were as varied as the programs and clientele they were designed
to serve. OEO, DOL, and the Department of Health, Education, and Welfare (HEW) were all involved in planning and
funding various programs. The goals and clientele that each
was designed to serve and the potential conflicts that these
programs encountered are seen in Table 1.

MDTA

The federal legislation that had the most impact on employment service was MDTA. The initial act was based on the assumption that technological changes were eliminating jobs for the unskilled and creating high-level jobs for which qualified applicants were lacking. Originally, the MDTA emphasized the selection of applicants who could acquire the vocational skills that would match them with jobs that were known to be available. "Institutional" MDTA training courses were initiated only when potential employment opportunities were certain and when unemployed workers who could be trained were present. Once these conditions were met, the employment service and local educators sought federal funding for training costs, equipment, and stipends for the trainees.

The early experience gained under the MDTA by local officials showed that the program was designed for the wrong group, as those displaced by new technolgoy often found their own jobs. Beginning in 1963 a series of amendments expanded the program to cover the unemployed, disadvantaged youths, and older workers. In 1966 the MDTA was redirected nationally so that 65 percent of its training effort was oriented to serve the hard-core unemployed; the remaining resources were restricted to helping train for skilled shortage categories. Other amendments liberalized payments and authorized more basic institutional programs.

The funding for MDTA programs was $70 million in 1962; this rose to approximately $142 million in 1970. The local recipients of MDTA funds were the employment service and state vocational, education, and rehabilitation agencies. Although MDTA funding of federal manpower programs continued to increase through 1971, the early emphasis on institutional training declined after 1966. More emphasis was put on work experience, on-the-job training (OJT), and work support programs (Table 1). These programs began to get priority because of the lower cost per trainee. However, because of the high demand for training of the poor and the limited resources of the act, MDTA was not by itself sufficient to remedy the problems of the hard-core unemployed.

EOA

EOA was another attempt to improve the delivery of manpower services to the disadvantaged. As Table 1 shows, this act was the most ambitious of all the manpower programs. It alone accounted for eight new programs, each serving a different clientele. Although these programs shared the same goal, they were at times overlapping, conflicting, and uncoordinated. EOA programs duplicated DOL's programs in the employment service, and the net result was that primary purposes gave way to secondary ones. As program after program was added to those already in operation, agencies pursuing the same goal ended up competing for the same clientele and the same jobs. Yet EOA, as a new agency, developed new ways to improve services to the poor, creating a range of programs for poverty communities. In the manpower field the three initial programs were the Job Corps (assigned to the OEO), the Neighborhood Youth Corps (DOL), and the Adult Work Experience program for welfare recipients (HEW).

EOA was amended almost every year. In 1965 Operation Mainstream was added to the act to provide training programs for chronically unemployed poor adults. In 1966 two new programs were added: New Careers and Special Impact. The New Careers program provided training for disadvantaged youth in paraprofessional and subprofessional jobs in community service occupations. The Special Impact program sought to involve private industry in the antipoverty effort. The 1965 and 1966 EOA programs relied on a variety of local delivery systems, particularly community action agencies. For most of these programs, the administering department (OEO) contracted directly with local community groups or other sponsors, some of which were formed specifically to run a local program. These groups, in turn, were responsible for subcontracting with various local agencies for the required program components.

USES was involved in these EOA programs in several ways. For example, local USES offices were charged with the recruitment, screening, and referral of disadvantaged youths (sixteen to twenty-one year olds) for Job Corps centers. The centers were designed to equip youths from impoverished homes with the skills and attitudes needed to find and hold suitable employment by providing them with basic education and prevocational training. As another example, the local employment service offices participated, through their referral activities, in the Neighborhood Youth Corps (NYC) program to help poverty-stricken youth remain in or return to school, gain work experience, and receive special training and other services. The local USES offices were also involved in the New Careers program authorized under the EOA amendment of 1966 (Table 1). This program sought to establish new and necessary community service jobs on a permanent basis, usually at the subprofessional level. New Careerists were trained to work in the employment service first as community service trainees and then as employment community workers and professional-level employment security officers.

In December 1967 several other important amendments were added to the EOA, greatly increasing the manpower focus of the act. One amendment authorized the Concentrated Employment program (CEP), an experimental effort designed and partially implemented by DOL in 1966. CEP was aimed at all unemployed poor individuals residing within defined geographic poverty areas; it attempted to bring together, under a single sponsor, the complete range of manpower programs and services needed to help such individuals become employable and secure permanent jobs. It is significant that the legislation authorizing CEP gave control of the program to public or private nonprofit agencies, not the employment service.[22]

In 1967 another EOA amendment encouraged the involvement of private industry in training the disadvantaged through a new business subsidy. Known as Job Opportunities in the Business Sector (JOBS), it provided direct grants to business firms to develop on-the-job training leading to specific job commitments for disadvantaged individuals. JOBS was an effort to place graduates of the various programs into jobs. To this end, it called on the newly formed National Alliance of Businessmen (NAB), an independent, nonprofit corporation, to secure commitments from private employers to hire the hard-core unemployed.

EOA viewed community participation in the design and

TABLE 1

Manpower Legislation and Programs, 1960-68

Program	Year of Passage	Funding Agency	Local Recipient	Clientele	Program Goals	Potential Conflicts	Funding in Millions Year 1	1970
I. Manpower Development and Training Act (MDTA)	1962 amended: 1963 1966 1968	DOL	State ES, State Voc. Ed. Supt., Local contractors for on-the-job training	Job-ready 1966-68: Hard-core	Institutional and on-the-job training in skills for which there are jobs available	High level of support needed per enrollee	$70	$412 (est.)
II. Economic Opportunity Act (EOA)	1964	OEO HEW DOL	Community action agencies, other private and public agencies	Minorities, Hard-core, Poor	Job training and related services to disadvantaged	Competition with other federal agencies	—	—
Title IA Job Corps	1964	OEO (transferred to DOL 1969)	Administrators-businessmen, unions	Youth	Comprehensive training for disadvantaged youth	Hostile community groups, cost	$183	$247.8
Title IB Neighborhood Youth Corps	1964 amended: 1967	DOL	Local community groups who contract directly with the regional manpower administration	Disadvantaged youth	Part-time and summer experience for disadvantaged youth	Drop-out rate	$132.5	$308.1

TABLE 1 (continued)

Program	Year of Passage	Funding Agency	Local Recipient	Clientele	Program Goals	Potential Conflicts	Funding in Millions Year 1	1970
Title V Adult Work Experience	1964 (phased out with introduction of WIN)	HEW	Local welfare agencies	Welfare clients	Jobs for select welfare recipients	—	$101	—
Title II New Careers	1966	DOL	Local public and private agencies, community agencies	Youth, adults—disadvantaged	Train disadvantaged for new careers in needed service jobs	Salaries, attitude of employees, other employes in agency	$36	$67.4
Title II Operation Mainstream	1965	OEO (transferred to DOL in 1967)	Local community corporations and business	Adults—Hard-core	To provide unemployed with work experience in public benefit jobs, such as beautification	—	$36	$51
Title ID Special Impact	1966	OEO (transferred to DOL in 1967; back to OEO in 1969)	Local community corporations and business		Involve private sector in concentrated economic poverty areas	—	$20	$46

TABLE 1 (continued)

Program	Year of Passage	Funding Agency	Local Recipient	Clientele	Program Goals	Potential Conflicts	Funding in Millions Year 1	1970
Concentrated Employment Program (CEP)	1967 amended to EOA	OEO (delegated to DOL in 1968)	Community action agency prime sponsor; state ES delivers manpower services	Hard-core disadvantaged in target areas	Broad range of job training and supportive services provided to disadvantaged living in target poverty areas	Competition with ES, community groups	$78.4	$187.1
Job Opportunities in the Business Sector (JOBS)	1967 amended to EOA	DOL	Special mechanism—National Alliance of Businessmen—created to set up local programs; tied in with ES	Hard-core disadvantaged veterans	Involve private sector in on-the-job training followed by job commitments	Lack of jobs, lay-off policy by employers	$24.3	$147.5
III. Social Security Act of 1967 Work Incentive Program (WIN)	1967	HEW DOL	Local welfare agency refers candidates to local ES office	Welfare clients	To provide intensive job training, basic education and supportive services to welfare recipients in AFDC category	Implementations, job market, ES and welfare personnel, ES as enforcement agency	$33	$78.8

Source: The National Urban Coalition, *Falling Down on the Job: The United States Employment Service and the Disadvantaged* (Washington, D.C., 1971), 29–34.

operation of the programs as essential to their success. The
OEO manpower services staff were advocates for the client in
each phase of the program. The client—not the employer or the
economy—came first.

Initially, the involvement of community action agencies and
other community groups was a significant challenge to the
employment service. It posed the threat of a separate competitive system that might corner the growing manpower funds,
which by 1965 substantially exceeded the Wagner-Peyser funding of the employment service. The OEO programs disre-
garded rigid civil service regulations and hired individuals
from the community better able to communicate with manpower program clients. Unlike the employment service staff,
these individuals formed a new and enthusiastic group without
loyalty to old norms or allegiances to professionalism.

Funding for the various OEO programs was extensive.
Initial funding for the Job Corps was $183 million, and this
increased to $247.8 million in 1970. The Neighborhood Youth
Corps had a first-year funding of $132.5 million in 1964, which
increased to approximately $308.1 million in 1970. Funding for
New Careers, $36 million in 1966, reached $67.4 million in
1970. Operation Mainstream funding rose from $36 million in
1965 to approximately $51 million in 1970. JOBS funding was
$24.3 million in 1967; it had increased sixfold in 1970 to ap-
proximately $157.5 million. This substantial growth in the
JOBS program meant that increased funding went to private
employers, primarily to supplement the on-the-job progams
that were gaining favor with federal administrators.[23]

NAB-JOBS

NAB-JOBS subsidized private employers willing to provide
jobs for the disadvantaged. From the beginning, there was a
conflict between the goals set for manpower agencies and those
for the private employers. In California, for example, while the
California Human Resources Department (HRD) and other
agencies believed that the goal was to help serve the disadvantaged, employers believed they were supposed to serve "qualified minorities." Seldom did the goals coincide. Yet NAB-JOBS

did pledge jobs to the agencies involved and, in some cases, provided jobs for applicants from these agencies.

CSES performed several functions within the JOBS program. It converted pledges into job orders, made referrals and placements, certified the eligibility of prospective enrollees, and published statistics on NAB-JOBS programs. Executives on loan from companies usually developed pledges from other employers and then turned them over to CSES, which converted them into job orders. Some pledges were not converted. Some employers, seeking ways to avoid hiring minorities, withdrew pledges when they found they involved hiring members of ethnic groups. Still others withdrew because of what they viewed as the referral of unqualified applicants. These employers rejected CSES as a hiring channel and turned to other agencies or methods to find employees.

The JOBS program was primarily a job development effort aimed at private employers. CEP, in contrast, was a coordinating mechanism that linked a series of components aimed at recruiting eligible persons, preparing them for jobs, and placing them in positions. As legislated, the two programs were completely separate from one another. However, none of the three CEP programs in the San Francisco Bay area was able to develop sufficient jobs for its enrollees. For this reason the programs were eventually forced to cooperate: CEP took on the task of making enrollees job-ready, and NAB provided the jobs. DOL regulations gave CEP preference for NAB slots. The natural link between the two programs had inherent conflicts, the major one being that NAB saw its mission as serving those from the top of the barrel, the CEP those from the bottom. In fact, few CEP enrollees got NAB positions. The link between the two was, therefore, spurious, and it survived only to the degree that it was specified in DOL guidelines.

The number of positions provided by JOBS was small. As of November 1970 the total number of positions developed in Oakland was 1,732 at a total cost of $5,298,151. In San Francisco the figures were 1,987 and $4,646,923. After 1969 pledges of jobs by employers increased, while hiring declined. On the average, a firm pledged about ten jobs, hired fifteen people, and retained 6.5.[24]

WIN

WIN, the last major piece of manpower legislation, was enacted in January 1969 as an amendment to the Social Security Act. Although it was originally under the sponsorship of HEW, program responsibility was soon transferred to DOL, where the secretary of labor delegated this responsibility to the employment service. WIN was designed to provide intensive "employability development" to selected welfare recipients in the Aid to Families with Dependent Children (AFDC) category. Its primary purpose was to establish a program utilizing all available manpower services, including those authorized under provisions of other laws. Individuals receiving aid under AFDC were to be given incentives, opportunities, and necessary services for employment in the regular economy and their participation in special work projects, thus restoring their families to independence and useful rules in the communities.

Employment service offices played a crucial role in WIN. After a WIN enrollee had been referred to an employment service, the enrollee was given professional guidance in establishing job goals and in determining a course of action. In addition to the employment service's counseling, testing, and referral, WIN also included program orientation, basic education, training in communication and employability skills, work experience, institutional experience, on-the-job training, job development, special job placement, and follow-up services to assist participants in securing employment with opportunities for advancement. WIN, in effect, made the employment service the center of a comprehensive manpower program.

The problems of WIN were rooted in its complexity: It had to cope with handicapped clients, a poor labor market, unfavorable economic conditions, and the lack of trained personnel and institutions equipped to deal with these problems. WIN was perhaps the most ambitious of all federal manpower programs, and, although more flexible than the other programs, its overall goal—reducing the welfare rolls—was also the most difficult. This was particularly true in a state like California, where the welfare benefits were relatively high. If WIN was to replace welfare or take people off welfare rolls, then the jobs had to pay more in wages and benefits than welfare did.

WIN funding was approximately $33 million in 1967; it increased to approximately $78.8 million in 1970. Expenditures through 1971 for the three bay area counties of Alameda, Contra Costa, and San Francisco were over $11 million. There were 7,329 slots available in these counties, at an average cost of $1,611 per slot. In 1970 the three counties spent $5 million and had only 272 "successful completions." Thus, the cost per completion was approximately $10,119. Out of a total of 7,329 persons, 727 had successfully completed the program.[25]

CSES: CHOICE AND CHANGE

For thirty years the employment service had served the needs of employers. It had sent them the best qualified applicants. Its staff had developed a sense of pride and professionalism in their work. Although they had discriminated against minorities, staff members were reflecting the mores of the time. They saw themselves as faithful and loyal civil servants carrying out the duties assigned to them as best they could.

In the 1960s social conditions changed, and the employment service was asked to change with them. Trained as it was to work with one clientele—the job-ready—the shift to another clientele—the disadvantaged—that it was ill-equipped to serve placed the agency in a vulnerable position. Most people find it difficult to change old habits; the employees of the employment service were no exception.

Another problem for the service was the expansion of its role to include areas of social policy. Not only had it become linked to the disadvantaged, but also it found itself at the center of a vast network of new programs, each calling for assistance; in many cases it was criticized for inappropriate responses and ineffective implementation. The problems did not stop here. The agency was damned by the politicians as noncreative, slow, disloyal, and unresponsive. Clients were hostile because the service failed to get them jobs. Other agencies objected to its

Figure 4
The CSES Network

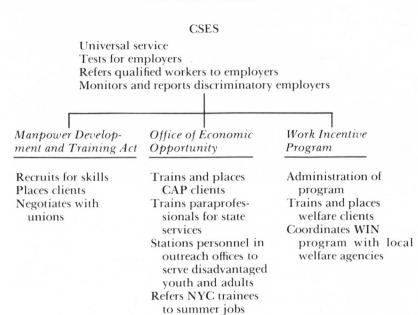

CSES

Universal service
Tests for employers
Refers qualified workers to employers
Monitors and reports discriminatory employers

Manpower Development and Training Act	*Office of Economic Opportunity*	*Work Incentive Program*
Recruits for skills Places clients Negotiates with unions	Trains and places CAP clients Trains paraprofessionals for state services Stations personnel in outreach offices to serve disadvantaged youth and adults Refers NYC trainees to summer jobs	Administration of program Trains and places welfare clients Coordinates WIN program with local welfare agencies

central position in the manpower efforts. Minorities objected to its discriminatory hiring practices and lack of responsiveness. Finally, it was criticized by employers for sending unqualified applicants. With such a multitude of criticisms, the employment service found itself alone, with few allies to help bolster its wounded pride (Figure 4).

Organizational problems are not easily diagnosed. What appears on the surface to be the total recalcitrance of agency bureaucrats is seldom the complete picture. Most people believe "that when situations change, the expert knowledge of the bureaucrat spells trained incapacity."[26] The ability to change is indeed an important aspect of the problem, but like most problems its dimensions are often obscured by other considerations.

An important factor to remember is that agencies like the employment service cannot easily accomplish significant transformations in the economic and social structure of our society within a one- or two-year period. Yet that was exactly what was expected of the employment service. In piling one new program on top of another, politicians ignored the need to find or develop additional managerial skills at all levels of the agency; they overloaded the system.

The growing number of programs in the manpower field demanded an expansion of the system. The failure of some federal manpower programs did not totally rest on their false premises but rather on the assumption that state personnel had the capacity to absorb—and implement—all of these programs. This became especially crucial when the resources did not meet the demands they generated. The question is not how quickly an agency can expand what it is doing, but what alternatives will carry it ahead most rapidly, within its set of limitations.

For the employment service, involvement in the new manpower programs was crucial. Competing agencies threatened to divert funding from the employment service and challenged its expertise in the employment field. While most of these new programs were sponsored by other agencies, the Bay Area CSES ultimately became inextricably involved in their implementation, a function it could not properly fulfill.

Thus, the use of an existing instrument, the employment service, for new purposes led to the development of systemic obstacles to change. Such obstacles arise when programs expand too rapidly, when there are inadequate resources, jurisdictional disputes, rigid funding requirements, or the lack of intergovernmental agreement (cooperation). All of these characteristics were present in the employment service during the 1960s. Though the goals and priorities were essentially the same, conflict arose over the best means to achieve them.

Conflicts over goals naturally occur when some agency feels that other agencies are doing what it could do better and getting the money it formerly received. The conflict between CSES and OEO is a good example of what can happen under such circumstances. The specific conflict involved a jurisdictional struggle between two large public bureaucracies—DOL and the newly formed OEO. When the OEO was established to serve the poor and its funding began to overshadow that given the employment service by Wagner-Peyser funds, DOL and

CSES became concerned. The struggle was not over whether the poor should be served, but rather over which agency could do the better job, given the necessary resources (especially since the funding level had shown a tremendous increase). The struggle reflected what Matthew Holden, Jr., has referred to as the "imperialistic tendency of bureaucracies."[27] The conflicts had little to do with the attainment of goals. No one was opposed to them. It was a struggle for power—with the poor as bargaining counters.

NOTES

1. It is clear from a review of the literature on the Great Society programs that there were many reasons for the failure of these programs; however, the official view laid the blame on the bureaucracy. See, for example, Allen Schick, "The Trauma of Politics" (paper prepared for the annual conference of the National Association of Schools of Public Affairs and Administration, Syracuse, N.Y., May 2–5, 1976), 7–12. Another excellent review of the success and failure of the Great Society programs may be found in Eli Ginzberg and Robert Solow, *The Great Society: Lessons for the Future* (New York: Basic Books, 1974), especially 211–20.

2. Anthony Downs, *Inside Bureaucracy* (Boston: Little, Brown and Co., 1967), 2.

3. For an excellent discussion of the problems of implementation, see Jeffrey L. Pressman and Aaron Wildavsky, *Implementation* (Berkeley: University of California Press, 1973).

4. The best account of the history of the employment service is Stanley H. Ruttenberg and Jocelyn Gutchess, *The Federal-State Employment Service: A Critique* (Baltimore: Johns Hopkins University Press, 1970), especially 1–23. For a more recent history, see Sar A. Levitan and Joyce K. Zickler, *The Quest for a Federal Manpower Partnership* (Cambridge, Mass: Harvard University Press, 1974), 1–12.

5. Ruttenberg and Gutchess, *Federal-State Employment Service*, 7.

6. Peter Blau, *The Dynamics of Bureaucracy*, rev. ed. (Chicago: University of Chicago Press, 1963), 94–98.

7. Ruttenberg and Gutchess, *Federal-State Employment Service*, 7.

8. Ibid., 28–33.

9. Harold Seidman, *Politics, Position and Power: The Dynamics*

of Federal Organization (New York: Oxford University Press, 1970), 188.

10. Herbert Kaufman, *The Limits of Organizational Change* (University: University of Alabama Press, 1971), 9–23.

11. Items 3 and 4 are not specifically a part of Kaufman's categories, but they are also conditions under which resistance may occur.

12. Kaufman, *Limits of Organizational Change*, 20.

13. Ibid., 21.

14. Max Weber, *The Theory of Social and Economic Organization* (New York: Oxford University Press, 1947), 340.

15. Blau, *Dynamics of Bureaucracy*, 94–98.

16. Olympus Research Corporation, *Total Impact Evaluation of Manpower Programs in Four Cities* (Washington, D.C., 1971), 18, 3.

17. Ibid.

18. Blau, *Dynamics of Bureaucracy*, 1.

19. Aaron Wildavsky, "The Analysis of Issue-Contexts in the Study of Decision-Making," *Journal of Politics*, 24 (1962), 718. See also James G. March and Herbert Simon, *Organizations* (New York: John Wiley & Sons, 1958), 36–47, and Downs, *Inside Bureaucracy*, 59.

20. Stanford Research Institute, *Pilot Study of Services to Applicants* (Palo Alto, Calif., 1967).

21. Sar A. Levitan, *Manpower Programs for a Healthier Economy* (Washington, D.C.: Center for Manpower Policy Studies, George Washington University, 1972), 6. For a complete history of manpower programs in the Bay area, see Olympus Research Corporation, *Total Impact Evaluation*. For a history of the Adult Opportunity Centers and Youth Opportunity Centers, see J. M. Regal, *Oakland's Partnership for Change* (Oakland, Calif.: Department of Human Resources, 1967). For a discussion of federal spending in Oakland, see Amory Bradford, *Oakland's Not for Burning* (New York: David McKay Co., 1968).

22. In many instances, however, the CEP sponsors duplicated the service provided by the employment service, which led to a mandated reliance on the employment service for certain services.

23. Although President Nixon had frozen all other manpower funds for 1973, he indicated that the JOBS program would not be affected by his dismantling of OEO. See Oakland *Tribune*, Feb. 23, 1973, 21.

24. Olympus Research Corporation, *Total Impact Evaluation*, Ch. 20.

25. Ibid., Ch. 16.

26. Robert K. Merton, "Bureaucratic Structure and Personality" in *Reader in Bureaucracy*, ed. Robert K. Merton et al. (Glencoe, Ill.: The Free Press, 1952), 361–71.

27. Holden, " 'Imperialism' in Bureaucracy," *American Political Science Review*, 60 (1966), 943–51.

3

The Politics of
Administrative Reform

Reform of public administrative agencies is deeply embedded in the political process. While bureaucrats may seek to perpetuate their existence, they do not determine the conditions of their survival. The dependence of public agencies on the legislature for funds and authority links them directly to the political system. Thus changes in presidential or legislative priorities mean changes in traditional bureaucratic operations and procedures. We illustrated this point in Chapter 2 by showing how the development of new manpower policies and programs at the national level resulted in changes in the employment service's traditional services and clientele. We also pointed out how the tendency of policymakers to use an existing instrument for new purposes can limit the effective implementation of public policy. Like Jeffrey L. Pressman and Aaron Wildavsky, we found that where existing instruments are used without an adequate assessment of the link between the instruments and the new purpose, the result is likely to be a failure of the new policy objectives.[1]

In this chapter we illustrate the linkages between politics and bureaucratic reform. We describe how the struggle for control over manpower policy between federal and state officials resulted in undesirable consequences for the bureaucracy. The policy struggle involved not only the question of what tasks were to be undertaken but also the issue of who was to be served.

The struggle over manpower policy has national significance. First, the key actors involved were both important state, and later national, officials. Ronald Reagan was governor of California during this period (1967–75), as well as the unsuccessful challenger for the Republican nomination for president in 1976. His attacks on federal bureaucrats are well known. Robert Finch was then lieutenant governor of California; he later became secretary of health, education, and welfare and a top aide to Richard Nixon. Second, the conflict involved the relationship between powerful elected state officials and appointed federal bureaucrats. Third, it illustrated how state governments use federal relations to open up new policy choices and, using federal funds, develop fiscal innovations. Finally, the outcome of a struggle with the federal government by one state is watched closely by officials of other states. A victory by California officials might well mean a victory for other states—what Arnold Meltsner calls the "follow the leader" theory.[2]

In addition, the conflict over manpower policy in California raises two other significant questions: (1) Under what conditions are states likely to challenge federal control over policy? (2) What factors contribute to a state's success or failure in such a challenge? We argue that this conflict is part of a broader issue in American politics—the fluctuating pattern of power between the federal and state governments over who should control and administer national policies in the states.[3] A brief review of the national manpower system sets the stage for the confrontation that follows.

THE NATIONAL MANPOWER ARENA

The United States Employment Service (USES), established in 1933, is the most powerful state manpower agency, although it has functioned more under national than state direction. Prior to 1968 manpower policies generally originated from Washington, and federal bureaucrats, not state officials, dominated manpower planning, design, and implementation. Federal attention was focused on assuring that federal monies went to nationally identified needs. While the programs were administered by the states, policy was made in Washington.

One reason for the federal dominance prior to 1968 was the funding arrangements. Funds to support USES, as well as state unemployment insurance operations, were (and still are) allotted by Congress to the states from a special federal trust fund collected from employers' payroll taxes. This unusual funding arrangement aroused concern because budgetary control by the federal government did not lead to total administrative authority. Nor did the states have more than minimal control over the functions of the agency. For all practical purposes, USES was an island unto itself. Although under the jurisdiction of both the federal and the state governments, it was really never totally controlled by either.

Another reason for federal dominance was that USES employees adhered to goals set down by the bureaucracy in Washington; over time these goals became the professional norms by which the employees worked. Efforts to change policy or operations—by either state or federal officials—usually met with stiff resistance from the Interstate Conference of Employment Security Agencies (ICESA), whose function it was to lobby and protect the Federal-State Employment Service system. The arrangement is unique. ICESA is attached to the Department of Labor (DOL); its office space is provided by that department. Seldom is manpower policy formulated without ICESA approval. ICESA can veto any changes proposed by DOL or others and, as such, serves as a classic case of "bureaucratic clientelism," that is, ICESA does for DOL what the department cannot do for itself. In return for its support, ICESA is given veto power over policies that it deems detrimental to the employment service. The unusual funding arrangements and the unique position of ICESA officials in DOL act as constraints on state control of manpower policies.[4] Stated differently, the establishment of what may be called a "trans-federal coalition" between state and federal bureaucrats limits state executive and legislative input at both the national and state levels.

The 1968 conflict over manpower policy in California is one example of the kind of tensions that are likely to occur between federal and state officials when one group is dominant. The California state government's effort to reform the state employment service was a direct challenge to the right of the federal government to control manpower policy. In other words, it raised the thorny issue of the distribution of power between federal and state officials. "When speaking of such fields as health, education, social welfare, and housing, the increase in federal government activities does not represent a shift of function in the sense of taking things away from the states; rather it means a new sharing of functions the states previously took care of alone. This may be less a matter of centralization in federal hands than the creation of semi-permanent tensions and a fluctuating pattern in the distribution of power as the two levels of government simultaneously cooperate and contend with one another for policy control and administration in these jointly operated areas."[5]

The federal-state conflict over manpower policy demonstrates clearly that despite the influence of federal funds—and despite the seeming power of the federal government to constrain state action—state governments remain partners rather than vassals in the federal system. We begin, then, by analyzing the California state government's efforts to reform the Federal-State Employment Service in California and the conflict that ensued between state and federal policymakers over manpower policy.

MANPOWER POLITICS IN CALIFORNIA

During the 1960s federal outlays for manpower programs increased thirteen-fold. In fiscal 1961 the federal government spent $235 million on manpower programs; by 1970 funding had increased to $2,596 million (Table 2). Clearly this was a decade of tremendous growth for manpower programs. By the end of 1970 DOL manpower programs alone had an enrollment of over a million (Table 3). The largest enrollment was in the Neighborhood Youth Corps, which focused on youth both in and out of school.

While funds and enrollments were increasing in the 1960s, the number of nonagriculture placements made by the public employment service suffered an almost continuous decline from

Table 2
Outlays for Manpower Programs
(in millions)

Program	Fiscal Year				
	1961	1964	1967	1970	1973
Department of Labor					
United States Employment Service	$126	$181	$276	$331	$431
MDTA-Institutional		93	221	260	358
Job Corps			321	144	188
JOBS				86	104
Jobs-Optional		5	53	50	73
NYC In-School			57	58	73
NYC Summer			69	136	220
NYC Out-of-School			127	98	118
Operation Mainstream			9	42	82
Public Service Careers				18	42
Concentrated Employment Program			1	164	129
Work Incentive Program				67	178
Public Employment Program					1,005
Program Administration, Research and Support	8	23	118	143	209
Department of Health, Education, and Welfare					
Vocational Rehabilitation	54	84	215	441	636
Work Experience			120	1	
Other Programs					
Veterans programs	14	12	19	141	291
Other training and placement programs	8	15	116	177	384
Employment-related child care	26	37	53	141	433
Total	$235	$450	$1,775	$2,596	$4,952

Note: Totals may not add up due to rounding, as the manpower programs were extremely fragmented and accurate figures were difficult to compile.
Source: Sar A. Levitan and Joyce K. Zickler, *The Quest for a Federal Manpower Partnership* (Cambridge, Mass.: Harvard University Press, 1974), 4.

6.7 million to 4.6 million annually.[6] The point here is simple: While more was being spent, fewer people were being placed. The decrease in placements was paralleled by the expansion of the total labor force at a rate of about 1.5 million jobs per year. Most of this expansion took place in urban centers.[7] The lack of placements and the high level of unemployment among the disadvantaged in urban areas led to criticism of the employment

Table 3

New Enrollees in Department and Labor Employment
and Training Programs
(in thousands)

Program	Fiscal Year			
	1964	1967	1970	1973
MDTA-Institutional	32.0	150.0	130.0	119.6
Job Corps			42.6	43.4
JOBS			86.8	51.5
Jobs-Optional and National OJT	2.1	115.0	91.0	147.5
NYC In-School		166.8	74.4	165.3
NYC Summer		227.9	361.5	388.4
NYC Out-of-School		161.6	46.2	74.7
Operational Mainstream		11.0	12.5	37.5
Public Service Careers		.0	3.6	24.6
Concentrated Employment Program			110.7	68.8
Work Incentive Program			92.7	238.5
Public Employment Program				177.9
Total	34.1	833.3	1,051.4	1,537.7

Note: Totals may not add up due to rounding.
Source: Sar A. Levitan and Joyce A. Zickler, *The Quest for a Federal Manpower Partnership* (Cambridge, Mass.: Harvard University Press, 1974), 5.

service by both federal and state officials.

In California these criticisms became the basis for reform. In 1968 most employed and underemployed persons in the state were located in urban areas. In this same year the state economy was flourishing, and unemployment for most groups (except the disadvantaged) was very low. (The national average was 4.0 percent; the state rate was 4.6 percent.) As a result of chronic unemployment in the midst of plenty, the state initiated efforts to reform the California State Employment Service (CSES), which for thirty-three years had been under the exclusive jurisdiction of federal policymakers. Any state encroachment into this area was certain to produce conflict with federal authorities.

By 1965 manpower programs had expanded so rapidly that California politicians became concerned not only about their widespread existence, but also about their political potential. According to a member of the state legislative staff, the legislature was the first group to recognize the profusion of manpower programs in the state. The legislature also discovered that the state had no control over these programs (except for the Department of Employment, which operated mostly on its own), and that none of them involved the legislature at all. Consequently, there developed a consensus in the legislature that some sense must be made of all the programs. Furthermore, the legislature considered this a productive area for state initiative. To this end Robert Singleton, formerly with DOL in Washington, was brought to Sacramento as a consultant to help interpret and evaluate the bewildering array of manpower programs.[8]

In January 1967 Reagan became governor of California; Finch became lieutenant governor. Finch and his aides began immediately to search for a project to keep him from falling into the empty drawer that is usually reserved for lieutenant governors in Sacramento. The question was how he could assert himself and have a policy role. Manpower policies were mentioned as a good project because (1) they had grown bigger and bigger since 1965; (2) there was considerable popular interest in the programs; and (3) manpower policies had no state direction. Finch became chairman of the California Job Training and Placement Council. Organized in early 1967 by the governor, the council was established by state law to be developed for the 1969 legislative session.

Finch and the Job Training and Placement Council expected that an additional year's work would be necessary to develop a coordinated job training and placement system. At that point, however, the powerful Speaker of the Assembly, Jesse Unruh, entered the arena. Speaker Unruh was the leading Democrat in a Democratically controlled legislature; as leader, Unruh opposed the Republican governor.

On March 21, 1968, Speaker Unruh announced in Detroit that he was proposing legislation to establish a new division within the Department of Employment. It would have sole responsibility for coordinating all job training and placement programs and for providing unemployed persons with necessary employment services. Unruh proposed the creation of a new kind of government employee to be known as a job agent. He stated that the job agent's work would be "defined by the needs of the people he serves, not by some civil service directive. This would be the job agent who would be given the responsibility of developing a job plan for the individual enrollee, contracting for the necessary services and seeing to it that the plan actually leads to a job. This approach, depending as it does upon individual initiative and responsibility, would provide a personal quality that is so sadly lacking in most government programs for the disadvantaged."[9] Unruh saw this as a way to assert or reassert state leadership in public policy fields dominated by the federal government. Furthermore, one of the tenets of Unruh's ten-year program was to build up the California Assembly's professional staff capability. His Detroit speech made it clear that he saw his manpower proposal as an excellent example of such an initiative. The speech also indicated that he was well aware that the initiative would require approval by the federal government, since most of the funds involved were federal. That Unruh's proposals were also purely legislative initiatives in an area previously dominated in California by the executive branch of government made them additionally attractive and satisfied one of the tenets of the Assembly staff system: the legislature should be independent of the executive branch and should be able to develop its own solutions to public problems.

Unruh's proposals caught Finch's group completely off guard. They also shocked the Reagan administration and Republican legislators who were working in the manpower field. The Republican leadership had minority consultants working on job creation proposals. In addition to preparing A.B. 109, the CAL-JOB Corporation bill, these consultants had developed A.B. 1966, to provide tax incentives for businesses to hire the disadvantaged, and A.B. 1777, to encourage participation in the CAL-JOB program by placing surplus state funds in participating banks.

The Reagan administration was also working on manpower proposals. In his January 1968 state of the state message, the governor had said that he would ask for the establishment of a Department of Human Resources Development, a proposal that had been developed by Health and Welfare Administrator Spencer Williams and his staff. As proposed in Reorganization

Plan Number 1 (1968), the new agency would be made up of (1) the state Service Center Program, consisting of seven multiservice centers, (2) the state Advisory Committee on Indian Affairs, and (3) the California Commission on Aging. At the time of this proposal, the first two were attached to the governor's office, the third to the Health and Welfare Agency. The new department would require *no additional expenditures; no substantive program developments* were proposed.[10]

The stage was set. An arena that had been empty of state political actors became crowded. Each group developed proposals independently of each other. In politics, as in other areas of our society, empty arenas will become crowded when the rewards are high and the costs are low. Politicians, in particular, seek issues that have high exposure and low political cost. In the developing manpower field, which is totally funded by the federal government, state politicians could liberally propose new programs and directions. Federal money opened up new policy choices and provided for fiscal innovations. But with so many actors in the same arena, could all improve their fortunes, or was it a zero-sum game?

Coalition Politics

Speaker Unruh's speech in Detroit paved the way for the development of a coalition. It was obvious that the speaker was moving into an area already carefully cultivated by Finch and that he was proposing legislation without consultation with or consideration for the Job Training and Placement Council and the manpower agencies already in operation.

Finch began the counterattack by issuing a press release pointing out to Unruh that the council was well on its way to making the "manpower training and placement programs more responsive to the special needs of the hard-core unemployed" and reminding him that "the legislature took action last year to do the job he proposed by establishing the council." Finch's statement received little press coverage, so Unruh's position was not threatened. This forced Finch to compromise and ultimately led to the formation of a bipartisan coalition.

Unruh's proposal to place the state Service Center Program[11] in the Department of Employment also caused considerable dismay among the people involved in the program. They felt (and indeed their suspicions were later justified) that the program, with its emphasis on providing one-stop service to the hard-core unemployed, would be rival to the employment service, which catered primarily to those ready to enter the job market.[12]

The Republicans decided that if anything substantive was going to be accomplished during the session, there had to be an accommodation and a bipartisan approach. The Speaker and his staff were approached by the Assembly Republican leaders and staff, and a meeting was held that resulted in agreement on a bipartisan legislative program. The agreement was then extended to include Finch and, later, Williams of the Health and Welfare Agency. Williams and his staff, it was believed, were very interested in a more ambitious program than the one contained in the governor's reorganization plan.[13]

When compromise occurs, groups are usually equal in power: To compromise is to recognize the relative power of others. In the political context, Robert Dahl has written: "Those groups that are less organized will lose; those that are either less resourceful, less affluent, or otherwise less effective get defeated. If the antagonists are more or less equal, there may be a stalemate or a compromise. Where different groups seek power relative to the other, each will seek ways to enhance his position or neutralize the other. Where this is not possible, coalitions are formed."[14]

Political compromise is a basic skill for most politicians. Indeed, it could be argued that the skills required for discovering and formulating the grounds on which coalitions can be formed, the assiduous and unending search for measures that will unify rather than disrupt an alliance, are the essential tools and skills of the politician.

The new coalition agreed that the speaker would be the primary author of a bill creating a wholly new Human Resources Department (HRD) and that the Assembly Republicans would have Democratic support for the CAL-JOB program and the other related job-creation bills. Also, to meet Republican wishes, it was agreed that the HRD bill (A.B. 1463) would

provide for contracts with private enterprises to offer manpower services.[15]

The coalition included all of the essential actors except
one—the governor. The governor's support was critical; to
move without his endorsement would have made the ambitious
effort much more difficult, perhaps impossible. Williams
became the key contact. He agreed to prepare a cabinet memorandum proposing that the governor enter the coalition. The
memorandum implied that Speaker Unruh had agreed to what
was simply a more ambitious form of the administration's
HRD proposal; it also suggested that a Health and Welfare
Agency skeleton bill would be the vehicle. It must have con-
vinced the governor, because shortly afterward he agreed to the
bipartisan HRD program. Issues that at one time seemed
irreconcilable came to be less so because one group could not
achieve its aims without the other.

The bipartisan legislative program was developed by a rare
and powerful coalition of political leaders during March and
April 1968 out of four essentially independent studies and
design efforts in the manpower field. On April 25 the Democratic and Republican leaders in the Assembly joined Finch
and Assemblyman Leon D. Ralph, chairman of the newly
created Assembly Subcommittee on Urban Problems, at a joint
press conference in the state capitol to announce the unveiling
of a "broad-scale revision and revitalization of California's job
development and placement programs."[16] On the same day
Governor Reagan issued a press release announcing his support of the program.

It became clear to the members of the bipartisan coalition
that if there was to be comprehensive action, their influence
over decisions on manpower programs had to be greater than
the influence exerted by any opposing coalition. The truth of
this assertion became critical when the plan was challenged by
DOL's employment service leadership and by labor organizations in Sacramento and Washington.

It is not enough to know who the primary political actors in
this drama were. Equally important are their reasons for wanting to change the old CSES. Normally, we assume that when
change is proposed there is a problem or that someone stands to

gain from the change. In this particular instance, there was not only a problem, but there were also potential political benefits.

The fundamental manpower problem, as stated by the sponsors of A.B. 1463, was the unemployment rate of the disadvantaged. In 1968 the national unemployment rate was 4.0 percent; unemployment in California was 4.6 percent. However, unemployment in urban poverty areas in the state was considerably higher than at either the national or the state level. For example, the Mission-Fillmore district in San Francisco had a rate of 11.1 percent; West and East Oakland, 12.0 percent; and south-central Los Angeles, 13.0 percent. The subemployment (unemployment plus underemployment) indices were 25 percent for Mission-Fillmore, 30 percent for East and West Oakland, and 33 percent for south-central Los Angeles.[17]

In a statement before the U.S. Senate Subcommittee on Employment, Speaker Unruh characterized the chronic urban-poverty area unemployment as " 'prosperity unemployment,' which is concentrated on those with few or no skills in contrast to the 'depression unemployment,' which occurred across the entire occupational spectrum and which dominated the consideration of social and economic policy. . . . That prosperity unemployment was qualitatively different and required different solutions."[18] Clearly, there were political advantages to be gained from serving the disadvantaged. There were also several other reasons why California politicians turned to this problem. First, most of the white middle class was already employed. Second, federal money was available in sufficient amounts that both Democratic and Republican leaders could offer something to their constituents. Third, the threat of violence added incentive to the push for a solution to urban poverty problems. But before politicians could offer solutions, they had to determine why existing programs had failed in the first place.

Why State Manpower Programs Failed

In an effort to answer this question, an Assembly Office of Research study group had identified twenty manpower programs in California. Their combined budgets amounted to $200 million. These programs were or should have been dealing with the urban unemployment problem. The study group uncovered a number of serious weaknesses in the system that prevented it from being effective.

1. There were no priorities for using the money available for dealing with urban unemployment; according to a principal Assembly consultant, some of it went to "housewives learning ceramics." The study group also found that, even though the Manpower Development and Training Act (MDTA) was shifting to serve the disadvantaged, less than half the enrollees were from minority groups.[19]

2. Most of the programs had rigid categorical limits that did not fit the multiple needs of the individual disadvantaged person. Often clients had to shop around for appropriate services and were forced to fit themselves into a program's structure.

3. There was no fixed point of responsibility for the delivery of manpower services. Since an immediate connection between training and employment was seen as a critical factor in program success, the absence of one person responsible for finding or providing a job for the trainee was a major weakness in the system.

4. There was no fixed point of responsibility at the state level. Many agencies had partial programs and partial sources of information. The separate programs often had different funding processes, and this was a source of confusion for the disadvantaged.

5. No meaningful research and evaluation was being conducted. Each of the programs had pieces of information required for an overall assessment, but no agency had a comprehensive supply of information. Evaluation was further complicated by the conflict between each agency's need to succeed and the handicaps of the target population. No procedures existed for evaluating performance "weighted by the disabilities of the client," and most of the programs did little or no follow-up to determine whether their trainees were successful. The little evaluation information that did exist suggested that there ought to be a shift from institutional training programs to on-the-job training with support services. However, there were no prospects under the existing arrangement for continuing evaluation of programs and policy alternatives.

6. There was a lack of jobs suitable for the disadvantaged, especially in the unskilled and semiskilled categories. Existing job opportunities often had entry barriers such as racial discrimination and credential requirements.

7. The general impression was that none of the programs appeared to work well.

These were the views of the Assembly Office of Research team and also of Speaker Unruh. The report made clear, however, that although the team members held these views, their major concern was with organizational issues. They were especially worried about the roles of the state Service Center Program and the Department of Employment. Although Unruh's initial proposals as announced in his March 21 speech would have created a new manpower division in the Department of Employment, the other participants insisted on the preservation of the state Service Center Program.[20] An agreement was reached that there should be a wholly new department, to be built on the service center model. Later this was to be changed because of opposition from DOL.

NEW PRIORITIES: NEW DIRECTIONS

Politicians need exposure. To capture headlines, they launch studies on problems of the moment and throw new legislative proposals into the hopper. They focus on proposals that will attract immediate attention, those that gain favor with their respective constituencies, and those that are congruent with their respective ideologies.

A press conference normally signifies a new direction or an attempt to explain or justify a previous decision or direction. The announcement of A.B. 1463 was typical of the way most new programs are begun. The bill as announced at the joint press conference is summarized below.

1. The state wanted to say where its priorities were. Priorities would be established for the use of pooled funds to ensure that those who needed the most assistance would get it. After the funds required for the Work Incentive Program (WIN) had been used, 85 percent of the remainder would be used in a set of

urban Economically Disadvantaged Areas (EDAs), where 20 percent of the families reported annual incomes of less than $3,000. Within the EDAs, the funds would be spent with first priority for unemployed heads of households, then for under-employed males between eighteen and forty-five years of age, and finally other unemployed and underemployed females between eighteen and forty-five years of age. DOL had deter-mined that 75 percent of these funds were to go to the disadvan-taged, but the state figure was fixed at 85 percent. A legislative staff assistant explained it this way: "Well, the feds were going in this direction, so we thought we'd just get ahead of them and push a little harder."

2. All programs should have not only priorities, but also more uniform management. Thus, there would be a single fund, the Manpower Development Fund, for the new HRD. It would pool federal and state funds from MDTA, the federal and state apprenticeship acts, the federal American Indian Employ-ment Act, the WIN program under Title IV-A of the Social Security Act, and the federal Adult Basic Education Program.

3. The new HRD would be the single state agency responsi-ble for directing and coordinating all manpower services in California.

4. The state needed research and information about the pro-grams because most of them had little follow-up, making it very hard to tell whether they were doing anyone any good. If some were, which ones were they, and why? If some were not, why not?

5. The key provision was that not only should the manpower system be tied together at the top by a unified system, but also that it should be tied together at the bottom, at the delivery end. That was to be the task of the job agents.

6. There was also to be a departmental Job Training and Placement Services Advisory Board with members from busi-ness, labor organizations, higher education, and the EDAs. The legislature and the governor were to make appointments, including a senator and an assemblyman, who would also constitute a permanent joint legislative committee concerned with the work of the new department.

7. Preferential treatment was to be given to the disadvan-

taged, just as preferential hiring was given to veterans.

A.B. 1463 was more than just an ordinary bill, for it was one of the few pieces of legislation that actually spelled out in detail what the duties of the job agent would be; thus, it impinged upon administrative prerogatives. It appeared that A.B. 1463 left no stone unturned and that no one could really oppose a bill designed to insure the rights of "the disadvantaged," "the poor," "the unemployed," "the underemployed," "the minorities," and the "hard-core." Who could oppose legislation of such obvious value?

Opponents did exist, and their existence led to conflicts between federal and state policymakers.

Conflict and Conciliation

The bipartisan coalition that was formed to pass A.B. 1463 included some of the most powerful people in state government: the governor and lieutenant governor, their top aides and agency heads, the Speaker of the Assembly, and the top leaders of both political parties. With such a powerful array of politicians, where would the opposition come from, and why would people oppose such a cause and challenge the state's most powerful leaders?

Opposition came primarily from two sources: DOL and its Division of Apprenticeship Standards (DAS) along with the division's labor supporters. DOL opposition was expected, not only because nearly all of the money involved belonged to DOL, but also because the career staff of the state Department of Employment would be affected. A twenty-two-page analysis of A.B. 1463 by the Department of Employment indicated that the bill in its original form would have transferred 1,781 of the department's 7,349 staff members (expressed as position equivalents) to the new manpower agency. According to the report, these positions were budgeted at $15,683,200. Coupled with $18,332,262 in MDTA training allowances, this would have resulted in a shift of $34,015,462 from the Department of Employment's $64.9 million budget. As one of the department's internal papers analyzing the bill said: "The transfer of these positions and funds would return the department to its traditional employment security service function which was its role before the advent of the manpower training programs.''[21]

The bipartisan coalition was instrumental in blunting the opposition of career bureaucrats. Although many of the participants attested to the intense opposition of career leaders in DOL, the department's official position throughout the legislative process was one of neutrality. Opposition to the bill through normal administrative channels was impossible because of the unprecedented agreement by Governor Reagan to join Speaker Unruh, Minority Leader Robert Monagan, and Lieutenant Governor Finch as co-sponsors of A.B. 1463. The only remaining administrative channel of opposition was through allies in the Bureau of Employment Security in DOL.

Speculation in Sacramento was that DOL would wait to see if the bill passed the lower house before mounting opposition. Advocates for the state DAS were more active in the lower house but were unable to muster significant voting opposition to the bill.

DOL mobilized its opposition after the bill was assigned to the California Senate Governmental Efficiency Committee. The assistant secretary of labor and manpower administrator, Stanley H. Ruttenberg, sent a long telegram to the chairman of the committee describing four major conflicts between A. B. 1463 and federal law and indicating that the secretary of labor would probably be forced to cut off federal DOL funds to California, estimated at that time to be about $600 million:

> (1) Federal statutes require that federal training and placement moneys made available to states be spent for the purposes for which they are made available and in accordance with the authorization and appropriation statutes; A.B. 1463 calls for commingling federal funds with state funds, and allocating such funds in accordance with state established priorities and determination. (2) The federal statute on employment service requires that service be given to all "men, women and juniors"; A.B. 1463 would limit placement services by any state agency to certain need categories. (3) Federal Employment Service statute also requires a single state employment service agency; A.B.1463 would create duplicating employment services. (4) Federal statues on unemployment insurance require offices, and that it be paid without regard to individual economic need: A.B. 1463's

provisions for employment services on the basis of economic need conflict with these requirements.[22]

The Ruttenberg telegram made clear that what was at issue was not the stated goals of the sponsors but rather their unstated goals. Ruttenberg knew that A.B. 1463 was a *direct* and *blatant* attempt by the state government to move into a policy area that had been and still was the prerogative of DOL. "State initiative" was a euphemism for gaining control over the Federal-State Employment Service and, with it, the power to control the funds for all manpower services in the state.

The telegram sparked a series of meetings between the legislative staff and Ruttenberg. The result was that the bill was amended substantially, with the most important amendments shifting the entire program back to the Department of Employment, renaming it HRD, and creating a separate manpower division within the newly named department.[23] In spite of the extensive amendments (the last of which was passed on July 1, 1968), on July 3 Robert C. Goodwin, administrator of the Bureau of Employment Security in DOL, spoke against the bill. He noted the large number of amendments and indicated that he and his staff had not had time to review them thoroughly but said that there was still substantial conflict with federal law and that California still risked losing federal funds.[24]

The state retaliated immediately. Following the hearing, Unruh, Finch, and Monagan issued press releases and letters condemning DOL for its opposition to A.B. 1463. One of the internal legislative working papers, "Federal Issues re Job Development and Training Package," stated that "Federal Officials informally indicated after the hearing that they were acting on orders from Washington to oppose the Bill." The paper also said, "Witnesses at the hearing admitted that the decision as to whether or not California programs were out of conformity with federal law was a discretionary matter with the Secretary of Labor. There is little doubt that the program would be affected if he were willing to allow it."[25]

Unruh called the DOL testimony a denial of the creative federalism espoused by President Lyndon Johnson and claimed that, despite a promise, the DOL representative had failed to address his testimony to the bill in its amended form. Finch followed by stating that DOL had used specious arguments and implied threats to oppose a central feature of the legislative package. Monagan indicated that California would continue to try to cooperate with DOL but warned, "If, however, you [Department of Labor] choose to obstruct our efforts, we may continue to be frustrated by bureaucratic waste and inefficiency, and our disadvantaged citizens will suffer the consequences."[26] U.S. Senator George Murphy likewise took DOL to task. In a Senate floor speech, he said that he was "shocked" by the high-handed manner in which DOL dealt with the state of California.[27]

Ruttenberg responded to each California leader and to Senator Murphy and asked that his reply also be printed in the *Congressional Record*.[28] Ruttenberg felt that the material Senator Murphy had put into the *Record* presented an inaccurate picture of DOL's position and activities and insisted that the *"department had supported the bill's stated objectives"* (emphasis added) to improve manpower services to the disadvantaged. He said that following Goodwin's testimony the department had continued to work with the California legislature and that on July 15, the day of Murphy's speech, Charles Odell and Curtis C. Aller, manpower administration officials, had gone to California to offer further testimony on A.B. 1463 on behalf of the department. Ruttenberg added that they had suggested other amendments that were accepted; he felt "that the framers of the legislation were satisfied with the results."

DOL was caught in a political bind. Some time between July 3 and July 15 Aller suggested to Ruttenberg that they call a halt to the conflict and do what they could to permit local initiative.[29] Both Aller and Ruttenberg resented being trapped in a position that was contrary to their expressed desire to encourage local initiative and innovations and to reorient the state employment service to serve the disadvantaged. The problem for Ruttenberg was that, while he favored local initiative, he could not back it as long as it was in conflict with federal law. The Wagner-Peyser Act was specific: federal funds could *not* be mixed with state funds, nor could there be two different employment services in one state. For the secretary, the issue was how to foster state initiative without violating federal law. It is ironic that Ruttenberg, later to write one of the most perceptive books on reorienting the service, was caught in a position that made him look as if he favored the status quo.

With the backing of the secretary of labor, Odell and Aller were sent as new DOL spokesmen. In testimony on July 15, Odell condemned "the legislative and executive branches of the State Government for moving so fast and so far in the direction of strengthening and pinpointing the effort to serve the disadvantaged by reconstituting the Department of Employment as a HRD and by singling out for priority treatment within the department the employability development and placement of the hard-core unemployed." He added that the department's concern was that A.B. 1463 as written might result in "a separate but equal kind of service to minority groups" that would be contrary to federal law. Odell said that there must be a single service open to all and that the Wagner-Peyser Act funds must be spent for job placement and counseling services. His statement continued:

> In contrast, the funds made available to the states under the Manpower Development and Training Act can be spent with considerably more flexibility, and the Act continues to be amended to permit the purchase of a wide range of employability development services. Our legal people have, therefore, proposed a series of specific amendments to A.B. 1463 which would on the one hand accommodate the requirements of the Wagner-Peyser Act for a comprehensive employment service and on the other hand for the flexibility in the use of funds contemplated under A.B. 1463. Specifically what they propose is that the Wagner-Peyser funds allocated to the State of California, including those for Youth Opportunity Centers, be used to fund employment and placement services, including the disadvantaged, as defined in A.B. 1463 and the funds available under the MDTA be pooled to provide the intensive employability development services contemplated for the disadvantaged *including the hiring of Job Agents* to act, in effect, as employability development specialists on a case load basis.
>
> If both these programs are organized and managed under the general direction of the Human Resources Development De-

partment, we see no problem in making sure, within the overall limitations of funds, that the placement needs of the disadvantaged can and will be met on a priority basis, but they will be met by a *single placement agency* which deals with all employers' orders and which assures that the disadvantaged are exposed to the *full range of job opportunities* available in the community at any given point in time. If more employment service staff needs to be deployed in target neighborhoods or service centers to give the disadvantaged priority attention, this can be done under such as setup. At the same time, the creative concept of the Job Agent as outlined in A.B. 1463 can be brought into play *to see to it that the disadvantaged get the services they need including proper and efficient job placement service.*[30]

Why did state officials accept these amendments? They did so because the trade-offs were in their favor. First, they were allowed to reorganize the agency, to appoint a new director, and to appoint three new top-level administrators who would be responsive to state direction. Second, state acceptance of HRD as the single state agency still meant that the state could establish a new jobs division that would give priority to the disadvantaged. Third, the compromise allowed the state to establish on paper a single state fund for all manpower programs. Conformance with federal laws was accomplished by simply setting up separate accounts for each program. Fourth, the state was allowed to hire 150 new job agents with MDTA funds. Fifth, the state was allowed to use 75 percent of all manpower funds for the disadvantaged.

In addition, the state was allowed to circumvent the Wagner-Peyser Act by simply transferring regular employment service personnel to HRD offices in ghetto neighborhoods. (Early versions of A.B. 1463 had called for the transfer of approximately $34,015,462, or 1,781 regular employment personnel, to HRD functions.) When this sum is added to the use of 75 percent of all manpower funds to serve the disadvantaged, the sum is indeed very large (Table 2).

Acceptance of DOL's amendments cleared the way for the bill to move out of the California Senate Governmental Efficiency Committee. The issue of future conformance with federal law was solved by providing assurance that any provision not in conformance would be inoperative.

The other major source of opposition to the bill. while not as publicized as the DOL opposition, was just as effective. The *California AFL-CIO News* claimed that the transfer of DAS to the new HRD department, along with the provision of A.B. 1464 (introduced by Assemblyman Ralph, D-Los Angeles), would "emasculate the California Apprenticeship Program."[31] Assemblyman Ralph's A.B. 1464 would have taken the authority to investigate complaints of discrimination in selection of apprentices away from the DAS and given that authority to the Fair Employment Practices Commission (FEPC).

The two bills passed the Assembly over labor opposition, although the *News* noted there were only eleven votes against A.B. 1463 and twenty votes against A.B. 1464. In the Senate labor opposition caused the elimination of the DAS transfer from A.B. 1463 and the amendment of A.B. 1464 to give DAS fifty-one days to settle a discrimination complaint before the FEPC could take over the case. Mike Manley, then legislative aide to Unruh, said that elimination of the DAS transfer from A.B. 1463 was not done for "political reasons." He added, "They [labor] just plain flat ass beat us on that. We couldn't get the votes to move the bill as long as the DAS provision was in it."

The compromise by DOL came partially from its own concern for strengthening services to the disadvantaged as well as from a belief in supporting local initiative. From the department's point of view, to support local initiative was one thing, but to permit intrusion by state officials into policy areas previously the domain of the federal agency was another. Given the concerted attack by both state and national politicians, however, the department was forced to compromise. The compromise resulted in the state's accepting the amendments to A.B. 1463 as suggested by department officials.

State officials won the battle, but they may have lost the war. By taking over the control and administration of manpower policy, they also assumed responsibility for the outcome—jobs for the hard-core unemployed. (And, as matters turned out, the state did not achieve this important objective.) The initial outcome of the state's efforts, however, may be summarized by looking at the final product—the Human Resources Development Act of 1968.

Human Resources Development Act of 1968

A.B. 1463 was signed into law as the Human Resources Development Act of 1968. Its primary provisions, both of which developed late in the legislative process, were: (1) the creation of HRD, reconstituted from the Department of Employment, which was to give first priority to serving the disadvantaged,[32] and (2) the elected officials of the state were to control the state employment service in California.[33]

Some aspects of the bill—such as the creation of job agent positions, the provisions for experimentation, the research and evaluation requirements, the advisory committee, and the priority for services to unemployed heads of households—were enacted as proposed. Other aspects were changed markedly. The title of HRD remained, but instead of drawing the manpower functions from the Department of Employment and building on the state Service Center Program, the seven multiservice centers were moved into the Department of Employment. The state Office of Economic Opportunity and the Commission on Aging were also made part of HRD, although DAS and the state Advisory Commission on Indian Affairs were dropped from the bill. The department was designated the "sole state agency to approve and coordinate publicly funded job training and placement programs," although the Health and Welfare Agency would be responsible for coordinating all state agency manpower programs. The chief of the Job Training and Placement Division within HRD was designated chairman of the statewide Cooperative Area Manpower Planning System (CAMPS).

Under this reorganization, the Health and Welfare Agency for all practical purposes controlled most of the federal funds coming into the state. The agency comprises the departments of social welfare, mental hygiene, rehabilitation, public health, industrial relations, youth authority, corrections, and health care services.

The reasons for the reorganization have since become clearer.

Manpower funds and employment services alone account for over $600 million annually. When the other budgets of the Health and Welfare Agency are added to this, virtual control of most of the federal funds was ensured, including decisions on where and how they were going to be spent.[34]

The title of the Manpower Development Fund remained in the bill, but like the departmental structure its substance was radically different. Rather than being a pool of all available job training and placement funds to be used to meet individual needs, the fund became essentially an accounting device, with each source of program funds having an individual account. Service to disadvantaged persons in EDAs still received priority for funds, but the proportion was reduced from 85 to 75 percent. The provision that gave preference in awarding state contracts to firms that employ persons trained under the HRD program was dropped from the bill. The win, loss, and compromise aspects of the struggle are listed in Table 4.

Table 4
Federal-State Conflict: Winners and Losers

Area of Conflict	Federal	State
Single placement agency	Won	Lost
Unemployment insurance to all	Won	Lost
Priority to disadvantaged[a]	Won	Won
Control of employment service by state officials	Lost	Won
Use of federal funds for state priorities	Lost	Won

[a] The federal government mandated that 75 percent of all manpower funds go to the disadvantaged; the state mandated 85 percent. In negotiations with federal officials, state officials accepted the federal figure, but also won the right to use 75 percent of manpower personnel to serve the disadvantaged.

Anticipating that issues of conformance with federal law might arise in the course of implementing the new law, the legislature added a provision that automatically held in abeyance any provision which might be ruled out of conformance by the secretary of labor or other federal officials. The inoperative period for such provisions was to last fifteen months, and the federal official making the ruling was requested to "document specific conformity, decertification or withdrawal of fund issues" in a public hearing to be held by the director of HRD. The sponsors of A.B. 1463 seemed not only to expect further conflict with the federal government, but also to welcome such conflict as a necessary condition for changing the current programs.

FEDERAL-STATE POWERS: A NECESSARY BALANCE

In government the great question is how to achieve the maximum use of resources with the lowest expenditure of funds. Politicians seek government programs that have the potential for high political gain and low political cost. The federal-state conflict over manpower policies in California illustrates how state officials sought to gain, while making the federal government lose. But in politics, winners frequently end up as losers. For example, while the state won the battle to provide service to the disadvantaged, in the end it lost when it failed to provide jobs for this group.

This chapter has illustrated several broad principles of American politics. We have demonstrated that conflict over policy between federal and state officials is likely to occur in policy areas with large expenditures. We have also shown that when politicians in large states like California coalesce, federal officials are forced to compromise. Thus, federal policymakers may be forced to include state policy innovations in national programs.

This chapter also makes a more important point about the federal system—the fluctuating patterns of power between two levels of government. When a policy area becomes important to state officials, policy formulation, implementation, and design become issues for negotiation. Instead of federal dominance, sharing is called for; if this is not forthcoming, political pressure is brought to bear. In our example California's political leaders, party leaders, and congressional representatives united to exert pressure on the federal government. The result was that federal policy was changed.

Where state officials are responsible for the administration of national policy and where national policy conflicts with state priorities, strategies can be designed by state officials to convert possible losses into gains. This is especially true when the state stands to gain and the federal government stands to lose. In California the reorganization of the employment service was not a question of the efficient delivery of services to the disadvantaged, but rather of who would ultimately control the development of policy and the determination of priorities. Reorganization, then, was a means, not an end. The issue was power, not efficiency. State officials used the disadvantaged as bargaining counters with federal officials; the real issue was control of public policies.

Even if federal officials agree with state initiative, they cannot permit states to violate federal laws. Federal compromise ensured that the disadvantaged would not get "separate but equal" service; the compromise also ensured that California's new agency would cooperate with the national employment service. While the officials circumvented federal policies to permit state initiative, they did not violate them openly.

Finally, although it is important for federal officials to support local initiative, this does not imply that the federal government should abandon its role as the primary policymaker. Indeed, the federal government can no more abandon this role than state government can abandon its responsibility to its citizens. What this means is that where federal policy can be better implemented by state policymakers, the federal government should support the state. Cooperation by federal officials becomes a mechanism that facilitates local initiative without abandoning national goals or direction.

In the federal system, then, power does fluctuate and does create tensions. Federal power over policy does not mean dominance, just as state initiatives do not result in state supremacy. As power continues to fluctuate, cooperation between federal and state officials becomes essential. However, cooperation between these officials does not mean the absence of conflict. Rather, cooperation is a means of managing conflict when interests are partially in agreement and partially in disagreement. Cooperation is a process of continuous mutual adjustment, not the administration of settled policy. In the final analysis it is the mutual adjustment of interests that allows both the federal and the state governments to serve all citizens effectively.

NOTES

1. Pressman and Wildavsky, *Implementation* (Berkeley: University of California Press, 1973).

2. Meltsner, *The Politics of City Revenue* (Berkeley: University of California Press, 1971).

3. Recently some scholars have argued that revenue-sharing has made this type of conflict moot. That seems highly unlikely for two reasons: (1) Revenue-sharing has not eliminated other categorical programs run by the federal government, nor is it likely to do so in the near future. (2) While at present revenue-sharing gives more flexibility to state and local governments, changes by Congress could lead to more stringent guidelines in the future, thus reviving the likelihood of federal-state conflict. In addition, conflict is likely to develop in such fields as education and transportation as new federal laws demand more than most states are willing to concede. The Reagan administration's block grants program may reduce tensions in some areas but is likely to increase them in others. The issue over who should fund welfare costs, the federal or the state government, is one such issue.

4. See Stanley H. Ruttenberg and Jocelyn Gutchess, *The Federal-State Employment Service: A Critique* (Baltimore: Johns Hopkins University Press, 1970), in which Ruttenberg advocates the reorientation of the service toward the disadvantaged. Among the barriers to such changes, he cites as one of the most potent the ICESA. According to Ruttenberg, the conference has lobbied Congress against proposed changes by DOL in manpower and employment laws and has succeeded in stifling federal intiatives. It appears that in some cases ICESA has served as a channel of opposition for dissident members of DOL who have opposed their own department's policies. The reverse situation seems to have developed in California, where some state employment service staffers were using DOL to try to stifle state initiatives. In the effort to pass A.B. 1463, many participants viewed the U.S. Employment Service as almost totally free of state control, and Ruttenberg describes the tremendous difficulties in directing the state agencies from the federal level. The state and federal viewpoints together cast the state agency as nearly an island unto itself, a very difficult proposition to account for in a modern democratic theory of government.

5. Michael Reagan, *The New Federalism* (New York: Oxford University Press, 1972), 18.

6. Sar A. Levitan, *Manpower Programs for a Healthier Economy* (Washington, D.C.: Center for Manpower Policy Studies, George Washington University, 1972), 6.

7. Ibid.

8. Unless otherwise specified, most of the comments in this section are taken from interviews or from a March 1980 unpublished report by the California Assembly Office of Research.

9. Jesse M. Unruh, "A New State Role in Providing Jobs," speech presented at the Conference on the State: A Current Appraisal and a Forward Look, Detroit, Mich., Mar. 21, 1968.

10. Ronald Reagan, "Reorganization of the Executive Branch of California State Government: Reorganization Plan No. 1 of 1968," Feb. 1, 1968, 37–40 (emphasis added). It is interesting to note that the governor's proposal stated no connection at all between the proposed Department of Human Resources Development (HRD) and the existing Department of Employment, although the proposal noted that the Department of Employment "has a special interest in the disadvantaged citizen, and its federally funded programs are specifically directed to the training and job placement of individuals from poverty areas" (36). Nor did the plan include the state office of the Office of Economic Opportunity in the new department of HRD (52).

11. The state Service Center Program was established by then Governor Patrick Brown after the Watts riots of 1966. He set up thirteen centers to help serve the hard-core unemployed following the issuance of the president's *Report of the National Advisory Commission on Civil Disorders* (New York: New York Times Co., 1968). Subsequently, in an economy move, Governor Reagan closed seven of these centers.

12. Developments since passage of A.B. 1463 confirm that this fear was well founded. The general social service orientation of the intake units of the centers have been almost eliminated in favor of an orientation toward manpower exclusively. The September 1972 reorganization removed the last few remnants.

13. It is not unusual for agency heads to seek more ambitious programs than those proposed by the executive. In fact, some agency heads are seen as the enemy to be watched by the executive and his staff. See, for example, Francis E. Rourke, *Bureaucracy, Politics and Public Policy* (Boston: Little, Brown and Co., 1969), 16–21.

14. Dahl, *Who Governs? Democracy and Power in an American City* (New Haven: Yale University Press, 1961), 202.

15. This is a perfect example of how consensus politics leads to the ambiguity of policy; it also illustrates the tendency to use an existing instrument to carry out new policies without assessing the relationship between the instrument and the new purpose.

16. Building the bipartisan coalition in the 1968 session was a political feat. There was built-in conflict during that session for many reasons, the most important of which was that 1968 was an election year. In the first three months of the year, before the coalition was formed, there had been divisive partisan conflict over the financing of Medicare, welfare, handicapped children's services, public education, tax withholding, and several less important issues.

17. The estimates are taken from DOL publications. A method for calculating subemployment rates is given in the *Report of the National Advisory Commission on Civil Disorders*, 257, 264–65.

18. Unruh, "Statement before the U.S. Senate Subcommittee on Employment, Manpower and Poverty Concerning California's Efforts to Reorganize Manpower and Job Training Efforts and Programs," May 10, 1968, 4.

19. The MDTA of 1962 was primarily concerned with the consequences of technology and labor displacement. It was conceived as a *retraining* program for skilled workers who were unemployed. By the time of the Watts riots, the focus was shifting, and MDTA was changing from a retraining program for displaced skilled workers to a program of initial training. At the time the legislature became interested, MDTA was just in the process of shifting.

20. According to the Assembly Office of Research, the new Division of Job Training and Placement in the Department of Employment would have drawn together such manpower functions as MDTA and the incoming WIN program and separated them from the main employment service and unemployment insurance payment offices. At that time these were grouped together in a Division of State Employment Offices and Unemployment Compensation under Albert B. Tieburg, who had been director of the Department of Employment under the previous Democratic administration.

21. California Department of Employment, Division of Administrative Services, "Department of Employment Staff and Funds That Would Be Affected if A.B. 1463 Is Enacted in Present Form," May 6, 1968.

22. Ruttenberg telegram to Senator Richard J. Dolwig, chairman, State Committee on Government Efficiency, June 6, 1968.

23. The debate over A.B. 1463 might have been substantially different if the Intergovernment Cooperation Act (ICA) of 1968, which permits waiver of the "single state agency" requirement, had then been law. Section 204 of the ICA states: "Notwithstanding any other Federal law which provides that a single state agency . . . must . . . administer . . . any grant-in-aid program, the head of any federal department or agency . . . may change provisions upon adequate showing that such provisions prevent the establishment of the most effective and efficient organizational arrangements within the state

government ... provided that the head of the Federal department or agency determines that the objectives of the Federal statute authorizing the grant-in-aid program will not be endangered by the use of such other state structure or arrangements."

24. "California Assembly Bill 1463: Testimony of Robert C. Goodwin, Administrator, Bureau of Employment Security, United States Department of Labor, before the California Senate Committee on Government Efficiency," July 3, 1968.

25. California Assembly, Office of Research, "Federal Issues re Job Training and Development Package," Mar. 1968.

26. Ibid.

27. *Congressional Record*, July 15, 1968, S8608-11. A summary of the California bills was also published in the *Record*.

28. The index to the *Congressional Record* shows no entry for Ruttenberg's letter.

29. Interview, Curtis Aller, May 20, 1972.

30. Testimony of Charles Odell, Manpower Administration, DOL, before the subcommittee of the California Senate Committee on Governmental Efficiency, July 15, 1968, 1-4.

31. *California AFL-CIO News*, May 31, 1968.

32. The amendment offered by Odell (U.S. Unemployment Insurance Code, sec. 11007) greatly broadened the impact of the bill by allowing all of the administrative resources of the Federal-State Employment Service to be used in serving the disadvantaged. As the HRD program developed, Odell's suggested amendment provided additional resources and thus gave the bill its true ultimate meaning. The job agents were paid with state employment service administrative funds, as were the assistant managers for client development; some new center facilities were also leased with these funds.

33. To carry out this intention, the bill provided for the appointment of two extra deputy directors exempt from civil service. Also, from its inception the bill contained a provision indicating that the legislature intended to maintain policy control over the program (U.S. Unemployment Insurance Code, sec. 9001).

34. This illustrates how state governments use their relations with the federal government to free federal funds for state use.

4

Bureaucratic Leadership and Policy Change

Structures are seldom permanent; they change as needs and priorities change. This is especially true if the external environment contains a great deal of uncertainty.[1] Though seemingly efficient and desirable at one time, structures can develop defects that call for new solutions. Since most reorganizations involve a long-term effort, it may take several years before an organization reaches a new symmetrical state. This was the case with the new Human Resources Development (HRD) reorganization.

The organizational structure adopted by the HRD administration at first seemed to serve its intended purposes—opening up a centralized structure and dealing with an uncertain environment. However, executives who initiate organizational structures rationally designed to cope with one aspect of uncertainty may in time find that they must develop new responses. Gilbert Sheffield, the first HRD director, was not ignorant of this need to remodel the organizational structure as needs arose. In September 1969 he wrote in the *HRD News*:

> If you move from a one-story house to a two-story house, your good old ladder probably won't do the job. That's the situation we're in today, as I see it. Our old ladder is still strong. It's got good rungs. But it can't reach where we're headed. So I'm trying to put together a ladder to meet our present need. With Phase I of HRD's plan to go into effect, I want nine months good service. If social and manpower problems grow, or change shape, or add a new dimension, then it's our job to develop a new plan, a new organization if necessary, to cope with that change. Another ladder.[2]

Social and manpower problems did change drastically between September 1969 and January 1971. An eloquent account of the shift in priorities was given by Floyd Edwards, shortly after he was appointed by the U.S. Department of Labor (DOL) as the new manpower director for the region that includes California. In April 1972 state HRD officials invited Edwards to address a conference that was not only aimed at improving federal-state relations but also supposed to signal a change in policy direction. The Edwards speech, given at Asilomar to all top-level HRD personnel, was deemed so significant by the director of HRD that a copy was sent to all agency employees.

The speech, "And Here We Are, Ten Years Later," has become one of the best known speeches in HRD history. It criticized both federal and state direction over the past ten years. Edwards stated that the Federal-State Employment Service had so diminished in effectiveness in the preceding few years that it faced possible extinction. The service had indulged in a world of abstract theories, prognostications, and clichés; with its head in the sand, it had refused to see what was happening around it. The public and Congress had grown more and more disenchanted with the service and, most important of all, so had the disadvantaged.[3] In short, Edwards believed that the employment service had gotten off the track and that it was time to admit it and get back on the track:

> Thirty-nine years ago, in 1933, the public Employment Service was created by the Wagner-Peyser Act. It was given a simple mission—to serve both workers and employers by getting people in jobs. An easily understood task and one not too difficult to implement. In fact, we performed it well for many years.
>
> For the next three decades life was simple, unsophisticated, and bereft of perplexing social issues. We operated our labor exchange program and placed millions of people in jobs.
>
> Then in the late fifties, the sky fell in on us in the form of a technological revolution. Most of you can remember the thousands of unemployed who descended on the local offices in the late fifties saying they were replaced by machines. In agriculture, in industry, and in business this was literally true. Almost overnight, or at least it seemed that way at the time, our long-standing policy of matching the man and the job was no longer

adequate. Our application files were swollen with qualified and skilled persons, but the machines could do their work better and cheaper. What were we to do with them?

The solution seemed fairly simple. Retrain them. Throughout the nation there arose a hue and cry for retraining programs. ES people were as vocal as any, and they were right. Something had to be done.

Accordingly, in 1962 Congress passed the Manpower Development and Training Act (MDTA). It gave us a new start. After thirty years of limiting ourselves to job matching, we had a new and additional mission. This was the first time the manpower program (such as it was back then) changed to meet the changing times. Boy, were we excited!

According to Edwards, the new mission that MDTA had thrust upon the employment service was shortly found to be faulty. It was based, he said, on a miscalculation of the needs. In 1962, when the act was passed, the concern was with skilled people whose skills had become obsolete. As it turned out, these blue- and white-collar workers were not the hardest hit. In most cases, they had enough education and savvy to merge into the changing economy. The real problem was the unskilled worker, the manual laborer. Machines had done away with ditch-digging jobs forever.

As more and more of these unskilled workers became unemployed, public and political sentiment was aroused. We began to invent names for them. First we called them the "displaced," then "deprived," then "disadvantaged." Each of these words has a slightly different meaning. It is very interesting to observe the shift in thinking from one word to another. We began with a mental image of the displaced as a strong, husky, muscular man with his shirt stripped off, with sweat on his back, and a shovel in his hand. He was independent, proud, and self-reliant. We ended the transition in thinking with an entirely different image. The more our thinking shifted, the more patronizing we became. We started talking about "those people" who, unlike us superior beings, need our help to ever amount to anything. We must reshape their thinking. We must motivate them. We must counsel them. We must make them like us. While we still thought of the displaced as the displaced, we adjusted MDTA to concentrate on them rather than the white and blue collared. We set about to train them in a skill, since a skill was necessary to compete in the labor market. It was sound thinking and constituted the second time manpower policy shifted to meet changing needs.

The proliferation of manpower programs, Edwards pointed out, was sorely needed. The deficiencies lay not in the programs but in how the programs were matched to the problem. He noted that ten years after MDTA was born, the manpower programs were ten times larger, but the effects were the same. John Smith still wanted a job, and he had none; the objective, Edwards stated, was to get him a decent job.

> What have we accomplished in ten years? There are those who say that we have accomplished a great deal, that we have pro-vided motivation and drive, that we have penetrated the indi-vidual's psyche and imparted to him a new self-image, that we have remolded the person and made him over, that we have created new and better people. I say baloney. I say that if we have not found a job for John Smith, we have done nothing. I say that if we take a black kid off the streets of Watts, promise him the moon, and then drop him right back on the sidewalk six months or a year later, still without a job, it would have been far better for him if he never heard of us to begin with. I say that we have gotten so carried away with our own bumbling, amateurish attempts to be sociologists, psychologists, and general all-around do-gooders that we have committed the greatest sin of all. We have stopped listening to the very people we are doing all the talking about.

The speech emphasized the point that the employment ser-vice saw itself as an amateur psychologist and that it was attempting to turn the disadvantaged into middle-class workers. "The truth is that we have not been in the job placement business for several years now. We have been in the manpower massaging business. We have not been devoting our energies to getting people a job; we have spent our time partaking of social theory. And all the while, our house has been burning down around us." Edwards said that the employment service's job was placement, and, if the placement rate continued at its present level, it would be down to zero in two years. The employees were asked to consider the logical consequences if this were allowed to happen.

Edwards asked, "What do the disadvantaged want? How can we help him?" His answer:

> I have talked to many of them in recent months, and I have listened to them. It is surprising what one learns when he listens. What do they want? A decent life for themselves and their children. Translated into more specific terms, they want gainful employment, which in turn makes for education, housing, and all the other things that all of us in this room take for granted. The many John Smiths I have talked to told me they want a job. They also told me that they are sick to death of all the talk and no action and that they are totally fed up with being treated as nonpersons.
>
> There it is, our mandate to get people into jobs. You are the ones to get us back on the right road. There is no one else.

Edwards made two promises to the participants. First, he said, this was not another flash-in-the-pan priority like so many they had seen in recent years. It was genuine, he said, and it was permanent; we were indeed beginning to find ourselves in the manpower business. A manpower policy really existed at long last. Second, he promised that managers would have the opportunity to manage with the least possible degree of bureaucratic interference. He also added that the new HRD director, Sig Hansen, made the same promise.

The conference at Asilomar was an obvious attempt by Edwards and Hansen to shift HRD's direction. For some, it was too little too late. The "year of the turn-around" was indeed an attempt by both political executives to get the agency back on the right track, as they saw it. It was a signal of new policy changes; it was also a way of telling agency leaders that the governor's first priority, welfare reform, was also to become their top priority. The renewed emphasis on placement suggested that the organization would be destroyed if it could not achieve this goal. The renewed emphasis on the employer was the final signal that the agency was returning to where it had been before the initial reorganization in 1969.

While he was still director, Sheffield had received a proposal from his two deputy directors for a new organizational structure that would shorten their span of control and give adequate supervision to the fifty-three regional offices. Governor Reagan had indicated his interest in welfare reform, and the signal from the federal government indicated a need to return to placement. The new structure was designed to facilitate both tasks.

Proposals to reorganize existing structures in most agencies are easily predictable. Harold Seidman argues that members of governmental agencies have an instinctive need to reproduce the organizational system with which they are familiar.[4] New recruits adapt, after initial orientation, to the structures of the old.

The proposal to Sheffield was designed to diminish the amount of responsibility that the deputies had to bear by adding a new position, that of area administrator. As proposed by the two regional deputies, each deputy would have four administrators; each administrator would be in charge of twelve agencies. These administrators would report to the deputy and provide daily supervision of the office and center managers. One deputy saw it this way: "Among the twelve offices there would be a mix; there would be a service center, HRD centers, and regular employment service offices. And so Sheffield bought into that, and I started phasing it in before we had the approval to do so."

The new structure was never fully implemented. Just as it was being phased in, Sheffield was replaced by Hansen as director. The plan was changed again; instead of the two deputies having four area administrators, one deputy was to be in charge of all eight and the other deputy was promoted "upstairs." To discover why the director did not adopt these plans as his own and how the governor came to choose one deputy over the other, it might be helpful to discuss the basis on which political appointments are usually made.

NEW LEADERSHIP: A PROBLEM OF SELECTION

Numerous factors are involved in the selection of a candidate for a high position. One is the direction the prospective executive wishes the organization to take, which depends in part on where the organization has come from. According to Philip

Selznick, the selection decision involves an assessment of the stage of development of the organization: "As organizations develop and new problems emerge, individuals who served the organization well in an early stage may be ill-fitted for the new tasks. Characteristically, this is not so much a matter of technical knowledge as of attitudes and habits."[5] In Selznick's view a creative person may be needed to develop and disseminate a set of policies for the organization and to secure implementation of those policies through appropriate staffing and operating procedures. When this task has been completed, however, another type of leader—a person who specializes in administration— should take over the reins. The selection of key personnel, Selznick writes, "requires an understanding of the shift in problems that occurs as the organization moves from one stage of development to another."[6]

Selznick suggests that the theory used by Machiavelli and W. Pareto should be examined more closely:

> In the latter's discussion of the "circulation of elites" we are offered the hypothesis that innovator types (the "Foxes") are needed to devise new programs and techniques. To be effective, these "Foxes" must be associated with more conservative, forceful elements having strong institution loyalties and perseverance. As the new system or institution gains strength and has something to defend, the "Foxes" become more expendable; and the "Lions" take over complete control, trimming innovations to meet the needs of survival. But this in turn may limit adapting to new conditions. The institutional problem is to keep a proper balance of the social types needed at each stage.[7]

From a different perspective, Robert Michels suggests that "where organization is stronger, we find that there is a lesser degree of applied democracy."[8] One might say that the "Lions" become conservers; this is especially true if their main goal is survival.[9] Selection of a successor (a "Lion") is usually based on several factors: (1) loyalty by the candidate to goals of the present regime, (2) the needs of the agency, and (3) the skills, personality, professional background, and training of the candidate.[10]

Alvin Gouldner has shown that the appointment of an outsider as successor gives the new appointee the advantage of not being hampered by old loyalties and of being able to view the organization more dispassionately than a leader who had been a long-term member of the organization. However, there may be resistance to an outside successor by workers and line staff. Such a reaction is what Gouldner calls the Rebecca myth: "Some years ago Daphne du Maurier wrote a novel about a young woman who married a widower, only to be plagued by the memory of his first wife Rebecca, whose virtues were still widely extolled."[11] As Gouldner points out, many former leaders are idealized by their workers when they leave, even though they may have been disliked while in office.

The purpose of developing theories is to explain reality. The theory suggesting that different stages in organizational development demand different types of leaders must now be tested to see if it clarifies the situation in the organization we are examining.

Sheffield was an innovator with good managerial skills; these skills were what the governor felt were needed to launch the new organization. Sheffield's ability to select leaders who could move HRD ahead was crucial; he also infused the agency with the new goals through effective use of the media. As an outsider, Sheffield was able to view the agency's problems objectively. He also successfully completed the planned structural changes and was adroit enough politically to avoid alienating outside interest groups. As a political appointee of the state, Sheffield joined California's governor, state legislators, and congressmen in the battle against DOL. Returning control of the employment service to elected state officials was his major contribution. When he resigned to return to private industry in June 1971, the governor reevaluated the agency before deciding what qualities he wanted in the new appointee.

Reagan chose Hansen, a former deputy in the employment service. Hansen, unlike Sheffield was an insider, skilled and knowledgeable in agency operations. His management philosophy was also different from that of Sheffield. Hansen ran a centralized operation in the state Tax Collection and Insurance Payment Division (TCIP), with headquarters in Sacramento. He was efficiency oriented, and the quality of his work was known. Reagan chose him because he felt his skills would be well suited to consolidate some of the gains that Sheffield had made and to direct the agency according to new priorities.

Hansen was officially appointed in August 1971. Before his confirmation by the state Senate, Hansen indicated a change in policy that prompted the anger of new minority employees and some legislators: he announced a shift in priorities back to serving the job-ready and employers. Minorities protested that this was a shift away from the policy mandated by the legislature. Some legislators also questioned the policy change, and the new director's appointment was not confirmed for nearly two months.

The appointment of a new director is usually accompanied by a shift in policy. Hansen's appointment was no exception. His earlier statements on what he saw as the new directions caused concern among employees, especially the new minority employees. In September 1971 Hansen answered questions about his views for *HRD News*. Some of the queries raised and the answers given are instructive:

Q: Are you planning any specific changes in the Department's operational setup in Job Training Development and Placement (JTD&P) Division?

A: Yes, we are planning one such change, but some of the details have yet to be worked out. Essentially, under the reorganization, the two regional headquarters that currently exist in Los Angeles and San Francisco would be eliminated. This would result in more direct line supervision between deputy directors in Sacramento and operating managers in the field and should vastly improve and streamline the responsiveness of the JTD&P Division.

In addition, all staff functions in the JTD&P Division would be consolidated in Sacramento instead of being fragmented as they currently are, with staff functions split among staff sections in Sacramento, Los Angeles, and San Francisco.

As regards the present regional deputy directors, they would, under the planned reorganization, assume statewide functions instead of simply having regional responsibilities as they do under the present organization.

Under the reorganization, the northern region deputy director would remain a deputy director and become in charge of

education and training in the JTD&P Division with headquarters in San Francisco. In this position he would have
statewide responsibility for working with the Department of
Education and public school districts, particularly community colleges, to help develop a curriculum that would prepare students to be more responsive to the requirements of
the world of work.

The southern region deputy director would remain a deputy
director and assume a new position and become in charge of
line operations for the JTD&P Division with headquarters in
Sacramento. He would have statewide responsibility and
would directly supervise the operations for eight HRD
administrators, four in southern California and four in
northern California.

Q: Will there be any layoffs because of these changes?

A: There will be no layoffs, forced transfers, or demotions as a
direct consequence of any of these actions.

Q: In your recent policy statement, you listed the three major
goals of HRD as: first, helping the job-ready to get back to
work; second, helping the hard-core unemployed to self-
sufficiency; third, developing new systems to forestall technological unemployment. Are these three major goals in order
of importance, and can you be specific about some ways in
which you hope to achieve them?

A: No, I didn't attempt to give them a priority preference by the
order in which they are listed. They were assigned "first,
second, and third" because one of them had to come first and
one last. Actually they are of equal importance, and I hope
that all HRD employees will attach to them such equal
importance.

The essential thing is that these three major goals give us
objectives and help us keep on target as we strive on a day-to-
day basis to achieve them. But let me make the point here, in
the event the question may have arisen in the minds of some
of our employees, that I am totally dedicated to helping the
economically disadvantaged.

We in HRD must keep that spirit and see to it that we
continue to present opportunities in an aggressive way to all
economically disadvantaged citizens of California. However,

I'm speaking of opportunities, not special privileges. We are one department and we do have a useful service to perform and we're going to perform it magnificently.

However, it is of paramount importance that we do what we can, and do it immediately, to help the skilled job-ready workers, who are currently unemployed to get back on the job. These individuals are job-ready right now, they are by far the easiest to serve, and their full employment will help generate taxes to support efforts to continue to help the economically disadvantaged. And these job-ready workers, like all other segments of our society, simply want opportunities afforded them so they can take advantage of them. I'm confident everyone will agree that's a fair approach and one that all of us in HRD want to take.

This doesn't mean, though, that any one group of HRD's clients will receive special privilege over another. Equal and effective treatment must be applied to all in our continued efforts in "developing resourceful humans."[12]

The statement by the new director seemed to promise all things to all people. Anyone reading the statement was sure to be confused. The disadvantaged were to get priority, but so were the veterans and the job-ready. For the old guard, it signalled a change back to the more traditional system; for the new, a shift in priorities, with the disadvantaged as the losers. Administratively, the division was to be centralized, and new policies were to be instituted.

Recentralization

The shift back to a centralized operation should not have come as a surprise to agency employees. As a former deputy director of Unemployment and Disability Insurance, Hansen had run a centralized operation. He was comfortable with this type of structure. Under Sheffield, both regional deputies had been brought up to date on statewide policy in executive staff meetings held every two weeks. In these meetings, the two deputies would report on the progress and problems of the regions. One of these reported later that he felt Hansen and others never really understood the role of the regional deputy. He suggested that, although the central office was aware of activities being initiated in Sacramento, it was not informed or knowledgeable about the deputies' work in the field. Consequently, the deputy felt, Hansen was uncomfortable in a decentralized situation: "I'm sure that the central office bureaucrats could never understand what [the other regional deputy director] was doing was entirely different from the way I was doing, and they weren't in a position to say, 'You do it like him.' I'm sure that bothered the hell out of the director because who the hell is minding the store? And that's a legitimate concern—who the hell *is* minding the goddamn store for the state? And I think that sort of firmed up in the director's mind at the point that hell, they needed to be coordinated if we are to have a consistent statewide effort."

The subsequent reorganization by the new director recentralized the division. The deputy in the northern region was appointed to head a new statewide office—the Office of Education/Training Liason, with headquarters in San Francisco. The southern regional deputy was put in charge of all line operations for one hundred offices; the eight new HRD administrators reported to him in Sacramento. Each of these HRD administrators supervised from twelve to fifteen offices. One other significant change was made in the division: the deputy in the central office was empowered to head the new statewide efforts of the department. He reported directly to the director (Appendix C).

How did the new director decide which of the two deputies should be in charge of line operations? Did he choose on the basis of leadership styles? These questions are important because many people in the agency felt that the northern deputy was removed for going too fast too soon in his efforts at decentralization. That does not seem to be the case, however, for as the northern deputy pointed out:

> The new director felt that outreach stations were fine, but one guy should be making the decisions. I think it was for that reason. I don't think he was as well aware of the difference in the two regional administrations that many people are giving him credit for. I'm sure he wasn't. The director never offered me either the line job or this; had he said there are two jobs, one is operating all the offices in the state or one is this one; then I would have said, hell,

give me the one I have now, because it will make the biggest impact
on the whole state. It will make the biggest contribution that the
department can deliver because as long as the department deals
with 10 percent of the employers and 10 percent of the people who
are looking for jobs, in my view, it doesn't have a significant role in
this society. But that's what the employment service has done
historically. That's what HRD is still doing. Ninety percent of the
employers don't even talk to us. Ninety percent of the jobs, people
get themselves. They don't need HRD for that. Then there's the
question of how effective are the services that we provide for that 8
or 9 percent through the manpower programs that were dreamed
up by someone who doesn't really know what's happening at the
local level.

Hansen's response to statewide coordination, then, was the
recentralization of the division. The appointment of eight new
area administrators to report to the deputy director of line
operations was made official in September 1971. Among these
were two black and two Chicano males. Three females, two
blacks and one white, were named assistant administrators.

The appointment of the new area administrators was significant. For each administrator chosen from the new group
(Career Executive Appointment managers), an old CSES (California State Employment Service) person was appointed as
assistant administrator; the converse was true for the other
appointments. This pattern was pervasive throughout the
northern region. For example, the new area administrator for
the San Francisco area was a recent black appointee to the
agency. His assistant was a white woman who had been in the
agency for eighteen years. In Oakland the area administrator
was a white male with ten years of service in the employment
service; his assistant was a fairly new black female appointee.

Having completed the reorganization, Hansen invited all
managers, deputies, and central office staff to a meeting. The purpose of this meeting and its repercussions merit our attention.

Conciliation and Consolidation. New top-level appointments are a source of concern for agency personnel. Succession
at the top usually engenders tensions that must be resolved if
new goals and policies are to be implemented.[13] Two methods
are available to political executives to publicize their policies

and to relieve employee tension. The first is to make a major policy speech in a friendly environment with ample press coverage. The second is to call a conference of the leaders of the organization for the purpose of uniting them behind the new goals. Hansen did both. His policy statements were made in Sacramento and published in *HRD News*. A conference at Asilomar, involving the top leadership of the agency, was designed to unite these people behind the goals of the new regime.

The Asilomar conference was conciliatory. As one minority manager said, "The word was sent down from Sacramento that there were to be no caucuses at the meeting. Controversy was to be downplayed for the sake of unity." The conference had three main themes: (1) unity and more involvement in welfare reform, (2) emphasis on working more closely with the employer, and (3) new emphasis on placements as the critical variable. Unity has a good ring, but it can be seen as a way of softening the blow that is to follow. The emphasis on welfare reform was seen by some as the major reason for the conciliatory stance taken by the administration.

Reorganization had already taken a great deal of HRD's time and energy. Although Hansen recognized this, he indicated that more changes were inevitable. But he promised that organizational change was to take a back seat to the real HRD objective—getting people jobs. One participant saw the conference this way:

> I think their primary objective in the central office was to heal wounds and really build the spirit of cooperation and unity. They did everything they could to keep controversy down. The last two annual conferences were very controversial. There was none of that this time. And they did everything they could to see to it that it stayed that way. And I do think in a way we are coming together, after two to three years of pulling apart. CO [Central office] opened the conference with general comments. The director spoke then and said that we've experienced a lot of change at the agency, but we're going to be in for more change. He dubbed fiscal year 1973 as the year of the turn-around, and that theme and phrase were used repeatedly at the conference. The feds used it; CO people used it. And the turn-around is to get away from the organization and to reach our objectives as an

agency. *And our objective is to get people working.* The other theme of the conference was the fact that we are going to work more closely with employers. We're going to regain the confidence of the employer (emphasis in the original).

Although the unity theme was heard frequently and broad goals were proclaimed, the same participant felt that the ends seldom equaled the means. He felt that there was a lot of pontification but very few facts, a lot of theory and well-meaning phrases but few practical suggestions. For example, the introduction of a new model, the comprehensive manpower organization, was an attempt to provide different levels of service: self-service to the job-ready and help for the disadvantaged. But few new resources were provided. The culmination of the conference was the new director's statement that the agency would be getting into the welfare business up to its ears very soon. Additional help for this new venture was not mentioned.

People call for unity when they want other people to believe as they believe. A call for unity is a signal that all is not well, but will be if everyone joins hands behind the chosen leader who will lead in the right direction. Hansen's call for unity signalled a shift in priorities away from the disadvantaged and back to the job-ready. Since new top-level appointments signal change, if one can interpret the signals correctly one is in a position to know what the changes will be.[14] The correct interpretation of signals is another way of gathering knowledge or intelligence.[15]

Following the conference at Asilomar, Hansen issued a statement to employers informing them that HRD was returning to the fold. In the letter, dated June 1972, he stated that the employment service had one purpose: to serve both the jobless and employers by getting people jobs. Hansen made it clear that the creation of HRD did not change the primary goals of serving the business community and the jobless:

In recent years we have been concentrating on helping the disadvantaged. Somewhere along the line, I believe we have gotten off the track with respect to recognizing your needs for productive employees at *all levels*. I say this, not only from my own observations, but from an accumulation of comments made to me by employers across the state since I assumed the position as director last August.

Some employers have indicated to me that whereas they used to look to HRD as a prime source for all levels of employees, they have in recent years been disappointed in HRD's response to their requests for other than the disadvantaged.

While we shall continue to help the disadvantaged person get back into the mainstream of self-sufficiency, I wish to emphasize to all employers throughout the state the importance I give to our responsibility to respond to your needs for *quality employees at every level*.

We must continue to give the veteran priority as we assist the jobless. We must continue to help the disadvantaged. But I want to emphasize to you that we are here to serve all people, at all times. We want employers to recognize this. We want employers to use our services more.[16]

The emphasis on welfare reform was Hansen's second major commitment. Newsletters went out to employers emphasizing dollar-for-dollar tax credit for employers hiring enrollees in the Work Incentive (WIN) Program. For example, a June 1972 newsletter outlined how employers could save 20 percent a year on their federal income tax by using WIN participants. The slogan was: "Give a hand, not a handout." Although the slogan caught on, the response from employers was not overwhelming.

In June 1972 a series of newsletters and bulletins stated that the employment service was experiencing an upsurge. One bulletin reported that after a discouraging five-year downward trend, the service was registering a "dramatic upturn" in both job openings listed and job placements.[17] This turn-around coincided with President Richard Nixon's order requiring employers with federal contracts to list openings with the Federal-State Employment Service. According to the same bulletin, "Since last October, listings have increased at an annual rate of about 550,000. Over the previous five years, decrease had been at the rate of about 150,000 a year."[18]

Secretary of Labor James D. Hodgson attributed much of this upturn to the mandatory job listing requirements, but said that the turn-around also stemmed from other factors, such as modernization of the employment service and expansion of the job bank system. He offered the following national statistics to justify his belief: "In the first quarter of 1972, 1,436,000 jobs were listed compared with 1,257,100 in the same 1971 quarter. For the six months from last October through March 1972, 2,821,000 jobs were listed—274,000 more than in the same six months a year ago. During the first half of fiscal 1972, 1,120,547 persons were placed a non-ag jobs, compared with 845,454 in the first half of fiscal 1971—a 37 percent increase."[19]

Hodgson said Vietnam veterans, who made up 5 percent of the nation's work force of 86.3 million, were also benefitting from the upsurge in listings and placements. The U.S. Employment Service placed 223,000 Vietnam veterans in the nine months ending March 31, 1972. The latest Bureau of Labor Statistics figures showed 3.9 million Vietnam veterans employed— 560,000 more than a year earlier—and 310,000 unemployed, no more than in May 1971, despite the quickening pace of military discharges. Hodgson also believed that employers were returning to the modernized employment service because it provided the largest single source of qualified workers in any community; its 2,300 local offices across the country were capable of interarea and interstate recruitment of workers. He further noted, "We are committed to maintaining and accelerating the recent gains. We have established a goal of thirty percent more job placements for fiscal 1973, and we plan to attain an increase of one hundred percent during the three years ending June 1975."[20]

In an address to the national conference of the Veterans Employment Service in Atlanta, Assistant Secretary of Labor for Manpower Malcolm Lovell stated: "Vietnam-era veterans made up nearly one-fourth of the total growth in employment in the past year, even though these veterans represent less than five percent of the civilian labor force. Five hundred and thirty-eight thousand Vietnam-era veterans found jobs in the last twelve months; they found those jobs while increasing numbers were being discharged from service—3.1 million between 1969 and 1971, while monthly discharges during early 1972 reached rates of more than 100,000 a month, and while draft calls were cut or suspended."[21]

Lovell attributed the success to: (1) the president's personal concern and leadership; (2) placement by the National Alliance of Businessmen of more than 97,000 Vietnam veterans in jobs in the nine months ending in April 1972; (3) the intensive effort of the president's Jobs for Veterans Committee; (4) the active support of mayors' and governors' committees all over the nation; (5) the opportunities opened up through the Public Employment Program (PEP), assuring compliance with the mandatory job listing requirement; and (6) the hard work of the employment service, which had not only halted a discouraging downward spiral in job listings but also accomplished a 65 percent increase in Vietnam veteran placements.[22] Thus, each upswing moved the agency back to its traditional stance, and each political appointee applauded this as a step in the right direction.

Another area of concern was the high level of unemployment among youth. In a speech on the need for intensified research on human problems, Hodgson addressed several questions to researchers: "What are we going to do about [youth unemployment]? The problem is a persistent one, and it has been getting worse for many years. Today the unemployment rate for sixteen- and seventeen-year-olds is almost five times the adult rate. For black teenagers, it is much higher. In 1971 the unemployment rate for all sixteen- and seventeen-year-olds was almost nineteen percent. For non-whites it was over 35 percent."[23]

With job placements on the upswing in California and across the nation, it would seem that things were going well for HRD. But that was not to be the case for its director. The governor was pushing for changes in welfare reform, as was Director Hansen, but the governor believed that if his new initiative was to be successful a person with closer ties to the business community would be needed.

A New Political Appointee: Another Shift

In May 1972 Governor Reagan appointed Dr. Earl Brian to succeed James Hall (who, in turn, had succeeded Spencer Williams) as secretary of the Human Relations Agency (the parent agency of HRD). Brian was thirty years old, a former flight surgeon in the Vietnam War, an author, and the chief architect of Reagan's massive 1971 Medi-Cal reform program. His appointment was effective July 1, 1972.

Brian commissioned a task force to study the needs of the agency, especially HRD. The new task force was headed by Gene Lynch, former Medi-Cal deputy. To no one's surprise, Lynch discovered that the department needed reorganization and a new direction—back to the old employment service concept.[24] The task force's recommendations were to have some new repercussions for the agency.

In September 1972 Brian appointed Lynch as a new deputy in HRD. Lynch was to report to both Brian and Hansen. Normally, a deputy reports only to the director; Lynch's role as Brian's appointee was a signal that Hansen's job was in jeopardy. The winds of change were blowing, but few knew when the change would come. As one employee said, "Task forces mean change, we know this. What we don't know is which direction it will take."

While the task force was busy conducting its probe, signals were constantly being sent out from Washington on what the new direction would be for the U.S. Employment Service. The key signal came from President Nixon in a report to Congress. On March 12, 1973, the *Wall Street Journal* carried the following headline: "U.S. Employment Service Switching Focus from Minorities to Supplying Skilled Labor."[25]

The report stated that the employer was back in the driver's seat at the USES. In a major policy "redirection" being spelled out publicly, the *Journal* stated, DOL was encouraging the network of state-operated employment offices to switch their primary emphasis back to lining up skilled workers for employers and away from the focus of the late 1960s on training and placing poor and unskilled persons. DOL officials asserted that the efforts mounted by the John Kennedy and Lyndon Johnson administrations to make the employment service a vehicle for placing disadvantaged jobseekers had not worked. The officials were telling the federally funded state agencies that "rebuilding responsiveness to employer needs is a key objective in all major labor market areas." Though the switch in emphasis had been hinted at before, it was spelled out with unusual candor in a report the president forwarded to Congress. According to the *Journal*, DOL officials also said that many employers perceived the local employment office as so preoccupied with services to the disadvantaged that they could no longer obtain referrals of any but marginally qualified workers at the lowest skill levels. Employers had become disenchanted in the mid-1960s, when emphasis was consciously switched away from USES's traditional labor exchange functions toward providing intensified and individualized services to client groups having the most serious problems in preparing for and holding a productive and self-supporting place in the job market.

USES was returning to the "trickle-down theory" of the job market. As the *Wall Street Journal* stated, "Federal officials argue that employers, worried about the skills and abilities of workers referred to them, simply grew more reluctant to list job openings with state employment offices. The new report says that while total nonfarm employment was rising about ten percent between 1966 and 1970, the Employment Service's placements shrank 30 percent and the number of placements of disadvantaged workers also fell. It adds: 'With fewer job orders, the ES experienced increasing difficulty in placing either the disadvantaged or the nondisadvantaged.'"[26]

The article went on to say that the employment service's total nonfarm placements were down to 3.4 million in the fiscal year ending June 30, 1971, from 6.6 million eight years earlier. It added that the agency was by then unable to serve very effectively either the job-ready or the disadvantaged, who needed "employability development." The primary reason given for the change was the Nixon administration's urgent need in 1972 to cool the fires of overall unemployment. In addition, the report stated, the renewed use of the employment service by skilled workers had also renewed employers' appreciation of the potential value of the service.

The statements by the president and high-ranking DOL officials signalled a new focus. But what of the disadvantaged? Officials stressed that the employment service would not abandon the disadvantaged jobseeker. But the report, signed by Secretary of Labor Peter J. Brennan, said that "an era of unin-

terrupted budgetary expansion for manpower training programs has ended, and selective reductions in effort will be
required in some areas and a leveling-off in others. Even the
drive to improve the general labor exchange must be shaped
with more attention to cost."[27]

State officials, monitoring the environment, often notice
what others do not; many times their political fortunes or
careers are in the balance. Brian seems to have received the
signal before it was formally announced. His reorganization
was to take advantage of the federal shift in focus and, with it,
the advantage of the use of federal funds. His next major move
after the task force report was predictable.

As Ed Salzman of the Oakland *Tribune* pointed out, extreme
alacrity was needed to rescue the state's job-finding agency from
total collapse. Programs launched by the federal government
and the Reagan administration four years earlier had almost
wrecked the state's largest department (13,000 employees in 140
offices). Job placements had sagged from 665,148 in 1966 to a
low of 282,521 in 1971 and 318,205 in 1972. HRD's job-training
program was generally considered a failure, and morale within
the department had dropped sharply. Moreover, there was
some threat that the federal government would withhold funds,
a threat that could not be ignored since the department received
80 percent of its $220 million budget from Washington.[28]

In March 1973, eight months after the task force report had
appeared, Dwight Geduldig replaced Hansen as HRD director.
Geduldig, a forty-nine-year old former Bay Area newspaper-
man, was no stranger to the department. His first job in state
service, ten years earlier, had been as a public information
officer to the employment service. When he was asked why the
HRD concept failed, he replied, "I don't really know. But I
suspect they were trying to peddle people who were not job-
ready." Geduldig further remarked, "We are not going all the
way back. But we are going to swing the pendulum back about
half way."[29] Geduldig also said that his greatest emphasis
would be on giving much more authority to the managers of
local offices. He explained that one general employment policy
does not work throughout the state, because each community
has a different economic profile. Since the federal government

allocated money separately for each program, Geduldig promised to go to Washington for a block appropriation so that his community management plan could be put into effect.

As Salzman pointed out in the Oakland *Tribune*, new efforts would be made in each city to coordinate departmental activities with local business and labor leaders. This was, he stated, an obvious attempt to win back the confidence that the state's economic community had once had in the employment service.

This phase of reorganization saw the old bureaucrats regain power in the agency. Every top spot was now held by people with employment service backgrounds. The HRD administrators were once again divided into urban and rural administrators, as they had been before reorganization. The minority employees and other HRD people who had formerly held high administrative posts were demoted to district supervisors.[30]

LEADERSHIP AND CHANGE

The appointment of a new political executive is normally a signal for policy changes. In the case of HRD every major new appointment signaled a change in the method of operation, and these changes were generally predictable. Each new leader gave clues about the directions he hoped the agency would go. In addition, task force members asked to raise questions and to offer solutions to ongoing problems also gave clues about the intentions of a new leader. Task force reports, in fact, do several things. Besides providing information about the new leadership, they inform new appointees about problems; inform agency personnel that changes are forthcoming; and inform the political executive and the public that a problem is being studied and that it will be resolved shortly. For bureaucrats, these signals are interpreted and passed on through informal channels where intelligence is gathered about the real objectives of the newly appointed executive. (The informal network among HRD managers was speedy and usually accurate.) Clearly, a large-scale change will be difficult, especially if it has to be accomplished in a short period of time. More often than not, these changes involve shifting priorities and conflicting goals. No one knows precisely what the rewards or punishments are for participation. Bureaucrats tend, therefore, to be conservative, sensing that today's priority may be tomorrow's fatality. Often they are wrong and resist for the wrong reason. But if the HRD reorganizations are illustrative, bureaucracies are able to remain relatively stable precisely because of this cautionary behavior and because bureaucrats know that few politicians remain for any length of time. The agency's personnel know or sense from experience that with new leaders come new goals and that while some changes will last others will not. It would seem that the ability to tolerate a high level of ambiguity is a necessary trait for those who wish to survive in a bureaucracy.

This last point needs to be emphasized and discussed further. Although it may seem to be a somewhat capricious element in our political system, it is nonetheless true that most high-level executive appointees have very short careers. They are men and women on the move. Moreover, the chief executives who appoint them occasionally have to dramatize their own activities by appointing persons whom they invest with superhuman qualities. These men and women rarely stay long enough to make a deep impact on the agencies they head. Thus, only rarely does a top-level appointee in a federal or state administration stay around long enough to get it on a stable course. This only adds to the problem of directing a constantly changing institution in a new direction.

NOTES

1. James D. Thompson, *Organizations in Action* (New York: McGraw-Hill, 1967), especially ch. 6.

2. *HRD News*, Sept. 1969.

3. *HRD News*, Special Bulletin, May 15, 1972.

4. Seidman, *Politics, Position and Power: The Dynamics of Federal Organization* (New York: Oxford University Press, 1970), 112-23.

5. Selznick, *Leadership in Administration* (New York: Harper and Row, 1957), 111-12.

6. Ibid., 112.

7. Ibid.

8. Michels, "Oligarchy," in *The Sociology of Organizations: Basic Studies*, ed. Oscar Grusky and George A. Miller; (New York: The Free Press, 1970), 28. See also Michels, *Political Parties* (New York: The Free Press, 1960).

9. The term "conservers" is adopted from Anthony Downs, *Inside Bureaucracy* (Boston: Little, Brown and Co., 1967), 96.

10. See Seidman, *Politics, Position and Power*, 98-135. See also U.S. Civil Service Commission, *Characteristics of the Federal Executive* (Washington, D.C.: Government Printing Office, 1968).

11. Gouldner, "Succession and the Problems of Bureaucracy," in *Sociology of Organizations*, ed. Grusky and Miller, 249.

12. *HRD News*, Special Bulletin, Sept. 2, 1971.

13. Gouldner uses the term "succession" to refer to the replacement of top-level people in organizations. See his "Succession and the Problems of Bureaucracy," 429-37. Grusky's use of the term refers to "succession" at all levels and not only top leadership. See Grusky, "The Effects of Succession," in *Sociology of Organizations*, ed. Grusky and Miller, 439-54.

14. I am using the word "signals" to refer to the way organizations monitor their task environment. The term is adopted from Martin Landau ("Decision Theory and Comparative Public Administration," Research Center in Comparative Politics and Administration, Brooklyn College of the City University of New York, 1967). It is somewhat analogous to what Richard M. Cyert and James R. March mean by the "search" procedures used by organizations. "Signals" differ from "search" procedures in that public agency heads, especially at the state level, take their cues from Washington. These "signals," if interpreted correctly, can lead to more autonomous use of resources with less dependency. For a review of search procedures used in organizations, see Cyert and March, *A Behavioral Theory of the Firm* (Englewood Cliffs, N.J.: Prentice-Hall, 1963). For an excellent review of the search procedures used in Oakland, see Arnold L. Meltsner, *The Politics of City Revenue* (Berkeley: University of California Press, 1971), 109-71.

15. For a discussion of how organizations get and use intelligence, see Harold Wilensky, *Organizational Intelligence* (New York: Basic Books, 1967).

16. *HRD Newsletter*, June 1972. Emphasis in original.

17. U.S. Department of Labor, Manpower Administration, *Manpower Technical Exchange*, June 23, 1972.

18. Ibid., 2.

19. Ibid.

20. Ibid., 2-3.

21. Ibid., 3.

22. Ibid., 3-4. Precedence to veterans had been and still was supposed to be the top priority of the agency. Formally it was; in practice it was not. In 1972 the president again made it the top priority by executive order.

23. U.S. Department of Labor, *Manpower Newsletter*, June 23, 1972.

24. Oakland *Tribune*, Mar. 12, 1973.

25. *Wall Street Journal*, Mar. 12, 1973.

26. Ibid.

27. Ibid.

28. Oakland *Tribune*, Mar. 12, 1973.

29. Ibid.

30. My formal research ended as the third reorganization of HRD was going into effect. The data on this and other developments come from newsletters, newspaper reports, and telephone conversations with friends still in the agency.

5

Structural and Administrative Decentralization: Strategies of Reform

Organizations are adaptive organisms; they respond to change due to internal conditions demanding attention or due to external events beyond the control of their staffs. In a public organization change is usually brought about by a disparity between what the agency is doing and what powerful critics—either inside or outside the organization—think it ought to be doing. Usually in such cases a new appointee is brought in. This individual is expected by his superiors and subordinates to find a way to reduce the disparity; in a few instances his appointment is based on the understanding that he will reorganize.[1] This obviously will involve one or another kind of change.

But reforming an organization is not easy. As Anthony Downs points out, the forces of inertia are always present and powerful in large organizations, since established procedures have previously involved enormous investments in time, effort, and money—a "sunken cost" of tremendous proportions.[2] Establishing new behavior patterns entails new costs. Therefore, organizations can rationally adopt new patterns only if the benefits expected from change exceed both the benefits derived from existing behavior and the cost of shifting to the new patterns. The more radical the change, the greater the inertia, and it will be greatest of all if the change involves altering the goals or the structure of the organization.[3]

Policymakers tend to use two strategies to reform public

agencies: they institute structural changes and introduce new incentive systems. Structural changes are politically motivated and redistribute the power of some officials; normally they involve changes in top leadership positions. A new incentive system is designed to change the way people are rewarded in the organization; it is usually aimed at changing the behavior of middle- and lower-level personnel. Both strategies have as their primary purpose the adaptation of the organization to new policy objectives. In this chapter our primary concern will be the effectiveness of structural change as a strategy of reform; the use of new incentives to effectuate change will be examined in Chapter 6. One way of illustrating the effectiveness of structural change is by analyzing how successful it was in reforming the traditional employment service in California.

A mandate from the California legislature set the stage for reform. The legislature not only authorized the governor to appoint a new director of the state employment service, but it also gave the new director a free hand and a honeymoon period for the implementation of organizational reform.

On June 1, 1969, Gilbert L. Sheffield became the first director of the California State Department of Human Resources Development (HRD). Sheffield had had a fifteen-year career with the Pacific Telephone Company, rising from staff assistant to assistant vice-president of personnel. Working out of the company headquarters in San Francisco, Sheffield was responsible for management training and developing programs, minority recruitment and relations, and urban affairs activities.[4] Ronald Reagan chose him because he believed that Sheffield would provide the vigorous new leadership needed to get HRD off to a good start.

The new director made several changes in the structure of the employment service. These changes included new top-level leadership; a new administrative structure; and the recruitment of new leadership and personnel at the middle and lower levels. The unique aspect of his strategy is that it did not rely only on top leadership to bring about the desired changes. The provisions for changes in lower-level leadership was the most innovative part of his structural strategy.

STRUCTURAL CHANGES

The legislation that mandated Sheffield's new position took the California State Employment Service (CSES), merged it with other state agencies responsible for working with the disadvantaged, created HRD, and carved out within the department the Job Training, Development, and Placement Division (JTDP). It was to that division that the legislation gave major attention. Sheffield's priorities also centered around the new division. His first decision was to change the leadership, and his first appointment was a new deputy to help plan and activate this component.

The new deputy, Ben Hargraves, had been in the Oakland public school system for twenty years before resigning to set up his own successful consulting firm. Why would a man who had spent twenty years in one bureaucracy join another? Sheffield's description of what he wanted to do with the new agency was persuasive. He had bold new ideas, a supportive piece of legislation, the authority to recruit new people, and the task of reorienting the department to serve the disadvantaged. After initially refusing the offer, Hargraves later reconsidered. His reasons were: "Well, when I started reading about the [employment service] and trying to think of the number of black guys who were in any positions at all, I found that I didn't know any. So I started to consider it more seriously. When I returned from vacation, I sat down with Gil and told him, 'Yes, I'll consider it.' I was appointed around the middle of August of '69 and was the first deputy appointed."

The ability of a leader to persuade and attract new appointees is crucial.[5] New leaders with new visions can attract people who seek innovation, especially when the goals of the organization agree with their own. Sheffield's offer combined status, money, and power—part of the necessary currency needed to attract and keep new people in organizations.

The new director had bold new ideas about how the department should be changed. His views, according to Hargraves, were exciting: Sheffield thought quite clearly that you change an organization by changing the leadership; to the degree that this can be done in civil service, in a state department, he wanted to do it. So he requested and received permission for more appointed positions than normally occur. He felt that he had to: (1) change the top leadership, (2) put decisionmaking down at the lowest point possible, and (3) decentralize the division in order to better serve the disadvantaged.

Sheffield decided that a centralized organization did not permit the amount of flexibility he needed to make the agency more responsive. Consequently, he reorganized the JTPD statewide by decentralizing it into northern and southern regions and appointed a deputy over each region with all of the authority the director of the department had. Hargraves became deputy of the northern region, and Lou Johnson was appointed deputy of the southern region[6] (Appendix C). The last major appointment in the JTPD was a new deputy to head the central office in Sacramento. Sheffield chose Dan Lopez, a former manager of the East Los Angeles service center. Lopez was responsible for the division's staff and for developing and assisting the regional offices.

With the major appointments completed, Sheffield established task forces to study and plan for the merging efforts. A task force is one way for new executives to find out what needs to be done in an organization.[7] The initial planning for the reorganization was done by Sheffield, Hargraves, and Allan Nelson, an assistant deputy to the director. Few others were involved at this stage of the preparation.[8] After the problems were identified, three task forces were set up to study them. All the members of these task forces were "insiders."[9]

One task force studied the staffing needs of HRD centers. Although the director accepted the reports on locations of centers, he pointed out that, "before proceeding with these recommendations, which would consolidate or relocate existing services, we are contacting local and other interest groups."[10] The director's decision to get technical approval or support before relocating was one way to avoid pressure from employers, unions, and other interest groups. Other task forces studied other areas. One was devoted to the development of training and employment plans as well as procedures for review, evaluation, and follow-up. Another study developed the layouts and estimates of space requirements for HRD centers. Reports were generated on HRD goals and objectives, the comprehensive area manpower planning system, the needs of and programs for eligible persons, and the allocation of funds. Other reports presented the needs for and ways to provide job information, an analysis of the characteristics of the unemployed and underemployed persons in each economic development area (EDA), and research into such areas as employee communications and public administraton.

Almost all of these reports were received ahead of schedule. Most of the people who participated in these task forces were later named to key positions in the organization. It seems reasonable to assume that task force members were chosen because of their public agreement with the new goals of the organization. Thus, these members tended to legitimatize what had already been decided upon by others.

Merger of the Old and the New

To establish a new agency is one thing; to merge an old one with a new one is another. With a new agency one can achieve a fresh start and bring in personnel who are supportive of new ideas. Traditions and past wisdom are missing; innovation is not a dirty word, and new people are less afraid to fail. But to build a new program with old people is more of a problem. Merging facilities is not extremely difficult, but securing the loyalty of the older agency personnel can be. Structural changes cause changes in roles and relationships among people in the agency; they also include placing personnel in new settings and situations.

Director Sheffield wanted to decentralize for administrative reasons. The legislation made it easy for him to do so because it quite clearly stated: "Services which are provided by the Job Training, Development, and Placement Division should if at all possible, be located where the disadvantaged live—the EDAs."[11] These areas were quite similar to the target areas set up by the Office of Economic Opportunity (OEO) at the beginning of the poverty program—Hunter's Point and Chinatown in San Francisco, and Watts and parts of East Los Angeles in Los Angeles.

The CSES had already established outreach offices in Hunter's

Point and West Oakland. Each of these Adult Opportunity Centers (AOCs) had a staff of about a dozen. Also in the same areas and sometimes in the same building, the Youth Opportunity Centers (YOCs) had another staff of similar size. As one interviewee pointed out, "The AOCs started in Hunter's Point as a project. The AOCs came out of the NAACP in Oakland working with the city and with the Department of Employment in the Adult Minorities Project—the Oakland Minorities Project. And the employment service provided the staff and that's why you have the Adult Opportunity Centers over in Oakland. You also had them in San Francisco. Richmond did not have them. They went in a different direction and instead of YOCs and AOCs, they had job upgrading offices and these grew out of Neighborhood House, which was stationed in the ghetto."

In the Bay area the merger was not an extremely difficult task. The same interviewee stated:

> So we already had a nucleus of a staff out there in the ghetto areas. It was a matter, then, of appointing a manager, rather than a branch manager, who had the authority for making decisions. Before, they had a branch manager who really didn't make decisions. They had to clear everything with the central guy. The same with YOCs. But it was a matter, then, in our plan, of combining the staff of the outreach YOCs and AOCs under one roof, appointing a manager, adding additional staff and adding also the newly created position of job agent in there so that each office would have a staff of close to forty.... So the biggest job we had was combining the staff, additional staff, civil service employment staff primarily, selecting a manager, and securing a facility that could be housed in the ghetto.

In places like Bakersfield and Stockton employment service offices were located in downtown areas that had become ghetto areas. Vallejo, Richmond, San Francisco, and Fresno had service centers, and East Oakland had AOCs and YOCs; these all remained as part of the new agency. The former deputy director of the northern region pointed out that the merger simply involved the combining of offices:

> It was primarily a matter of meeting with the newly appointed managers of the newly created HRD centers regularly to talk

about putting together a program. I encountered one problem in Oakland. Most of the people who work for the AOCs and YOCs thought that they were part of the poverty program. The employment service did not even have a sign on the building. They just had Adult Opportunity Center or Youth Opportunity Center, and many of their staff played a game about "Ain't it a shame what the bureaucracy is doing to you civil servants." So we really spent about two years training managers—not all of them had managerial experience—and clearing up the problems that existed before we merged.

Merging offices was only one part of the structural changes undertaken by the new director. The second part was decentralizing management and compensating for a lack of minority staff.

Decentralizing Management

The appointment of the regional deputy directors—two blacks and one Chicano—had been Sheffield's first step in decentralizing management. To be more effective in serving the disadvantaged, Sheffield separated the JTDP from the unemployment insurance and disability insurance programs. This was a major policy change, since all had been housed in one building, and the unemployment insurance division was more concerned with economy and efficiency than with serving clients.

The regional deputy directors were exempt from civil service. They replaced the old area managers and had more power in shaping policy. The operation of the regional offices reflected the new department's general decentralization policy, eliminating the detailed operating manuals and focusing on the individual centers and office managers as the key to development and supervision of the job agents and the Work Incentive (WIN) Program and other programs. As a former deputy said: "We were creating a new division and we really didn't have the manual ready, and Sheffield didn't want to use the employment service manual because the legislation quite clearly stated differently; if they had wanted to go that way, they wouldn't have needed the legislation."

The regional offices with their decentralized management had a totally different atmosphere from that of the old department. A consultant on manpower programs in the Bay Area noted: "Because of the policy of decentralization, the demise of operating manuals added to the emphasis on innovation. There is an important change in the concept of both staff and line operations at the regional office. There is far less concern now on insuring uniformity and conformity to manual instructions and considerably greater emphasis on providing technical assistance to field offices and stimulating changes and experimentation in the field."

There is no question that the staff of the regional offices saw themselves in a different role. They were to assist local field offices in their operations and suggest innovative ways to provide services to the disadvantaged. These innovations were later to cause conflict between central and regional office staff, as both strived to implement the new goals of the HRD.

The next step in decentralization was to compensate for a lack of minority staff by appointing career executive appointment (CEA) managers for the HRD centers. Under state rules CEAs were untenured management staff who held civil service positions immediately under appointed department leaders. They were to do whatever was necessary to achieve the department's objectives. Consistent with their status and the philosophy of decentralization, the HRD center managers were given a general management guide in place of the detailed manual used in the employment service. CEA managers were expected to make policy and to use the management guide with discretion in implementing departmental goals.

The CEA managers were on the same level as the district supervisors, who had supervised the managers of the old employment service offices. The CEA managers reported directly to the regional deputy directors. Although the division had been decentralized by setting up regional offices, the span of control was enormous. One former deputy noted:

> We had a dual system. We had CEA managers reporting directly to me. These centers were located in the cities where they had enough poor people. I had fifty-three managers in the northern region, and I think seventeen centers from Bakersfield and Stockton on up. It was a dual system because CEA managers reported directly to me, and the other managers [old employment service managers] reported to a district supervisor who reported to the

area supervisor who reported to me. So, for the managers of the downtown offices, or those offices that weren't HRD centers, that weren't located in the ghetto, they had two layers between them and me. And that was a dual system. I didn't encourage it. It just happened to turn out that way because of the HRD center managers being new needed more training than the old.

The CEA managers of the HRD centers had little experience. Only two had been a part of the old employment service. As one northern deputy pointed out:

> It was clear to me that the leadership at Hunter's Point should be a black person—that the leadership, the central manager at Chinatown should be Chinese so that he could speak the language; and that the Mission and Fruitvale needed to have Chicanos as managers. So many of my managers came from outside of the department because there were so few minorities inside. They came from FEPC, they came from rehab, they came from other state departments that had minorities at significant levels in supervisory positions. . . . We spent almost three years training these managers for the various positions to give them managerial experience to work with and give service to the disadvantaged.

In addition to appointing CEA managers, the new department compensated for lack of minority staff by bringing in job agents. Most of these were minorities, and by law they were to be located in ghetto offices. The initial recruitment of job agents called for 140 statewide. The first half had to be from civil service, and the rest could be from outside.[12] In the northern region, however, about 90 percent of the job agents came from inside civil service and had been the subprofessionals in the AOCs and YOCs. Because of their experience with the disadvantaged, they were promoted to the position of job agent. In Los Angeles most of them came from the outside. In both regions job agents received two weeks of training. The HRD center managers also took the job agent training because they wanted to know what training and guidance job agents would need to carry out their task.

A final area for minority recruitment was a new position in the HRD centers, the assistant manager, whose task was the supervision of the job agents. The assistant manager was not to be a traditional civil servant, i.e., he was not to come from the ranks of the old employment service staff. Instead, HRD administrators prepared a new examination to help select candidates. Moreover, HRD administrators felt that since the assistant manager would be supervising job agents and working with the disadvantaged, it would be better to have minorities in this position.

All of these new appointments meant dramatic changes in an agency that had had little minority staffing, especially at the middle and upper levels. Almost overnight the new agency had created a significant level of minority civil servants at the middle level (HRD managers), the supervisory level (assistant managers), and the lower level (job agents).

THE PROBLEMS OF IMPLEMENTATION

The new director moved swiftly to reorient the new department to give priority service to the disadvantaged. He successfully merged the staff of the old employment service with the new agency. He infused the agency with new top leadership. He decentralized management; increased minority staffing by bringing in minority managers in policymaking positions (CEAs); created new middle-level positions for job agents and assistant managers, most of whom were minorities; increased the supervisory-level staffing and integration of minorities into the agency; and communicated to the agency's personnel its new goals and priorities.[13] Both the governor and the legislature had given the new director the backing he needed to move the agency ahead, and its program started ahead of schedule.

The task of activation was carefully planned. Seventeen centers were to be inaugurated on a staggered schedule during November and December 1969, based on the availability of adequate facilities. The schedule of events included:

October 1   Transfer service centers to regional deputy directors

October 2   Begin to designate HRD center managers

October 3	Complete determination of availability of job agent candidates on promotional lists
October 6	Announce appointment of district supervisors
October 7	Designate HRD-center activation task forces for each region
October 8	Complete selection of initial increment of job agents from promotional lists
October 10	Announce appointment of unemployment insurance and employment service office managers
October 15	Begin designating activation teams for individual HRD centers
October 16	Complete selection of initial increment of job agents from open lists
October 20	Complete all personnel and fiscal documents to transfer positions, employees, and personnel funds for HRD activation
October 30	Begin employee orientation sessions throughout the state on HRD implementation
October 31	Complete transfer of all component employees, programs, and funds to HRD
November 3	Begin job agent training programs in Los Angeles and San Francisco
November 17	Begin assigning job agents and HRD personnel to HRD centers, service centers, and offices.[14]

Although off to a fairly successful start, the agency soon faced problems in implementation. The problems became more frequent as time wore on. Agency leaders had expected some resistance; they were not prepared for the amount that developed.

Reorganization involves planned changes. If we substitute

planning for reorganization, then we can say that planning is a process of preparing a set of decisions. Since a decision is an effective determination of policy, it involves a total process of bringing about a specific course of action.[15] Aaron Wildavsky offers a somewhat different definition of planning. According to him, planning is the ability to control the consequences of our actions. In other words, planning is the ability to control the future through current acts.[16] Since reorganization involves planned change, how can the planning organization help people to accept a scheme that will inevitably cause change? What preconditions and measures maximize the success of the implementation process?

Planning and implementation are part of the same process. If planning is the controlling of future events, what then does implementation mean? According to Webster's *Dictionary*, implementation means "to carry out, accomplish, fulfill, produce, complete." Implementation must have an antecedent. Before one can complete something, it has to be started. Policies are needed before programs can be implemented. As Wildavsky and Jeffrey Pressman have said, "Policies are theories. Whether stated explicitly or not, policies imply a chain of causation between initial conditions and future consequences. If x, then y. Policies become programs when, by authoritative action, the initial conditions are created. X now exists. Programs make the theories operational, thus getting into motion the causal chain linking the action to outcomes. Given x, we act to obtain y. Implementation, then, is the ability to direct the causal chain so as to obtain the desired results."[17] Implementation may thus be viewed as a process of interaction between the setting of goals and actions geared to achieve them. When programs fail to produce the desired result, the failure is often attributed to faulty implementation. What resources does a leader need to ensure that his plans get implemented?

Leaders need some way to ensure that plans will be implemented as intended. The legitimate use of power is one way to achieve this goal.[18] According to G. C. Homans, the main coercive resource of politics is the legislative process making the implementation of plans compulsory.[19] The translation of legislation into operational terms depends greatly on administrative machinery and on the implementors themselves. The effective power of the legislature is derived from its implicit threat to punish disobedience or from employment of force to ensure compliance. Consequently, the availability of such force, on the one hand, and the ability to impose the law, on the other, determine the effectiveness of the legislation. Although government generally does not monopolize the power resources available in society, it does have the exclusive authority to set the limits within which force may be legitimized.[20] Authority, according to Homans, suggests the notion of legitimate use of power.[21]

According to Wes Churchman, there are three basic strategies of implementation. The first is persuasion—selling of the plan by the tactics of good salesmanship. A measure of the performance of persuasion is the degree to which it attains acceptance. Next, Churchman identifies mutual education, which he defines as teaching the planners about the larger system and teaching the larger system about the plan. The measure of performance of mutual education will be the degree to which those involved in the implemenation process adapt appropriate roles to combine their knowledge.[22] The third method identified by Churchman is politics. This strategy involves identifying and changing the power structure of the organization. The measure of performance will be the reduction of resistance to the planning function, especially by reconstruction of political alignments.

It is much easier for a leader to apply specific rewards and sanctions to each operation when the goals are clear. Reorganization involves a great deal of uncertainty, however. Peter Blau presents several methods for coping with uncertainty. He argues that professional expertise, based in great measure on experience, knowledge, intuition, and creativity, is another way of assuring the reduction of uncertainty. Such expertise reduces the area of uncertainty by providing the knowledge and social support that enable individuals to cope with uncertainty and thus to assume more responsibility.[23] However, as we shall demonstrate, professionalism can become one of the problems, rather than a solution. By definition, reorganization involves changes in status relationships; it may produce serious morale problems among old employees, thereby reducing their loyalty to the goals and policies of the new administration.

Central Office Staff vs. Regional Office Staff

Reorganization of the old employment service included changed roles and relationships among individuals and groups. Decentralization into two regions meant that the central office staff no longer directed the functions of the regions. Sheffield anticipated some difficulty in shifting these roles and functions and therefore appointed a deputy to deal with this potential problem. As viewed by Sheffield and his two deputy directors, the role of the central office was to coordinate statewide efforts and to give supportive services to the regions. However, if both regional offices were autonomous, what was the role of the central office? Was it possible for a new deputy to change the roles, relationships, and behaviors of the old central office staff to reflect a new shift in policy?

Under the old system the central office staff had controlled and directed the operations of the CSES. At the outset Sheffield and his deputies were not concerned about the situation. By the middle of 1970, however, with regional staffs complaining about the central office and the central office complaining about the lack of coordination between it and the regions, it could no longer be ignored. The issue was forced by a former deputy who said, "The staff in Sacramento was still conducting business the way they had for years."

Sheffield discovered that the appointment of a new deputy was not enough. At a meeting he and his deputies began to outline the problems between the two staffs. A former deputy put it this way:

> [Sheffield] was recognizing at that point in time that having appointed me the deputy for the northern region, I had a chance to hire some new managers who would then be loyal to me—that sort of changed the leadership, but Dan really didn't have that opportunity. Gil then discussed the whole notion with Lou and me along with Dan and suggested that there needed to be changes in the chiefs in Sacramento so that there would be loyalty up there, so that they would know that it was a different ballgame. This must have been near the tail end of 1970—almost

a year—although we knew this all along it was how do we deal with it now.

The director's plan was that Lou and I would give up some of our managers and that these managers would be sent up to Sacramento, and the chiefs would be sent down to manage some of the HRD centers. They had about six chiefs up there that ran the section. Well, you can imagine how Lou and I responded to that, because we had just gotten our managers to the place where they were really putting together a program. Many of them were securing their facilities, establishing their local advisory committees, and this type of thing, but I could surely understand and see that this had to be a part of it, and so I contributed three of my managers to go up there as chiefs.

What had at first seemed a good solution turned out to be no solution at all. The strategy was to rotate chiefs in Sacramento out into the field and bring people in who would be loyal to the new deputy. On paper, Sheffield's plan may have looked good, but it did not work:

> Well, that didn't work because there wasn't a chief in Sacramento who couldn't find all kinds of reasons why they couldn't come. First of all, all of my offices except the service center in Richmond were Manager I classifications because of their size. The chiefs were really at the Manager II level. Although it was a different class, it sifted down to really one person, one chief who was willing to rotate. I will never forget one day when Gil called me and said, "Hargraves, can we back off of that? This guy keeps talking about dying or getting ulcers or something like that. . . ." So we backed off of it. So it only worked one way. We sent three chiefs up there, but none of them came out into the field.

Reorganization is useful in a number of ways. It removes unwanted personnel. Since the bureau chiefs would not leave, the bureaus were reorganized, and two new positions were created. Although one of the chiefs then left to join a consulting firm and another one retired, three of the old chiefs remained in office, and the new rotation policy was never implemented. As a result of the conflict between the central office staff and the regional office staff and the desire of the old chiefs to remain in Sacramento, a study was conducted to establish the functions of the central and regional offices. These functions are in Figure 5.

Figure 5
Problems of Coordination

Role of Central Office Staff	*Role of Regional Office Staff*
1. Planning program content and objectives for those areas affecting the state as a whole	1. Planning for the region
2. Policy setting in those areas where uniform statewide policy is required	2. Policy setting in those areas that are unique to the region
3. Developing and issuing minimum program guidelines	3. Setting regionwide objectives responsive to statewide objectives
4. Developing uniform procedures for those activities where uniformity of operations is necessary	4. Providing program support to the field offices
5. Coordinating statewide program activities and information	5. Implementing new programs
6. Distributing resources to regions	6. Where necessary, expanding minimum guidelines from the central office to meet the region's unique needs
7. Providing technical support to regions	7. Coordinating regionwide program activities and information
8. Contacting the federal government regarding program areas and serving as conduits for information to and from the feds	8. Providing feedback to the central office and field offices on program activity and innovations

Figure 5 (continued)

9. Preparing evaluations for the deputy director of the Job Training, Development, and Placement Division

9. Distributing resources to field offices

10. Designing needed legislative changes

10. Preparing evaluations for the regional deputy director

11. Developing statewide training programs in the division

12. Implementing the decisions of the director and the deputy director of the Job Training, Development, and Placement Division

In carrying out the above functions, central office staff will participate with regional staff to get their ideas and assistance. Central office staff will need to coordinate their activities among themselves.

In carrying out the above functions, regional staff will participate with central office staff to the extent necessary to prevent conflicts between regional policy and statewide policy and will participate with field office staff to get their ideas. Regional staff will need to coordinate their activities among themselves.

Communication Channels
Central office and regional office chiefs communicate directly with each other, by telephone, in writing, or in person, on program matters that are their responsibility. Similarly, central office and regional staff members, who report to the section chiefs, communicate directly with each other. This direct communication is not for the purpose of transmitting instructions. Instructions will continue to be transmitted through the line.

Source: *HRD News*, Special Bulletin, Sept. 8, 1970.

It does not take extraordinary insight to predict the difficulties that arose. For example, how can you coordinate at the state level and still allow the regional staff to meet the needs of the region? If the statewide office is to coordinate efforts but the statewide officer is equal in power to other deputies, whose decision will prevail? One might assume, then, that the decisions would end up with the director. If this should happen often, as is likely given the structure, an enormous amount of the director's time will be spent in solving disputes. What was clearly missing was the ability of the various groups to coordinate their efforts effectively.

Coordination. The term coordination is often used as if it had a commonly understood meaning. But, according to Harold Seidman, there is probably no word in administrative terminology that raises more problems of definition. At best, coordination describes both a process, the act of coordination, and a goal, the bringing together of diverse elements into a harmonious relationship in support of common objectives.[24]

Coordination is like peace. No one disagrees with having it, but few understand how to attain it. Wildavsky and Naomi Caiden assert that there are at least four important and possibly contradictory meanings for the term. First, they argue that when a common objective is sought, efficiency requires that it be achieved with the least input of resources. When these resources are supplied by a number of different actors, they must all contribute their proper share at the correct time to produce coordination. Under these circumstances, coordination equals efficiency.[25] The second meaning is the elimination of duplication and overlap that might result in unnecessary effort and outlay of resources. But, as Wildavsky and Caiden show, elimination of all duplication and overlap can result in failure. Redundancy increases the probability that an act will be performed or that a goal will be achieved. The larger the number of participants in an enterprise, the more difficult the problem of coordination and the greater the need for redundancy. Under these circumstances, coordination becomes another word for reliability. Third, when one person must induce another to do something that the second person would not do otherwise, coordination becomes a form of coercion.[26] Finally,

Wildavsky and Caiden argue that coordination of a policy means obtaining the consent of all the participants in the policy: "Bargaining must take place to reconcile differences, with the result that the policy may be modified, even at the cost of compromising its original objectives. Coordination in this sense is another word for consent."[27] Coordination then can be described in most cases as authority without power, a term which in fact covers up the very problem it is supposed to solve. Coordination is rarely neutral. Indeed, Seidman argues that it advances some interests at the expense of others. And regardless of the definition used, effective coordination is achieved only when it is advantageous to all of the important participants.[28]

What were the results of the efforts at coordination between the central office and the regions? The chief of the central office was to coordinate the activities of the division. Yet how this was to be done was not clear. Nor was it clear how the staff was to maintain a consistent statewide effort when the regions were autonomous. Part of the problem of the central office was the attitude and behavior of its staff.

> In a bureaucracy, such as ours, and I suspect this would be true in many of them, the central office has a staff of people, but they never behave as staff. They have behaved as operators, as making the decisions, telling the line what to do. You don't get it done that way. The people who know how to provide the services are the local guys in the office; not even the managers. The guys on that front desk who are in daily contact with the clients know what they need to assist them. So it means, then, that all the staff here—the staff in Sacramento—should be underpinning him; not telling him what the hell he can't do and all of that crap. And that is the biggest job the agency still hasn't addressed.

The regional deputies and their staff wanted the central office to be supportive, not dictatorial. The deputies agreed that the central office did handle one major function quite well— requests from the governor's office and from other agencies so that the local manager did not have to be involved in these matters:

> [Sheffield] handles it with his staff in such a way that it doesn't involve the time of the local office managers, and that is beauti-

ful. The local people never do recognize that. There are things coming in every damn minute of the day—some gripes from some citizens that go directly to the governor's office. Somebody has to put together a legitimate response. It is a time-consuming thing. And usually CO is able to handle it with the staff, with their merely getting on the phone and calling someone in the local situation to get a reading and to put together the report without sending it all the way down and involving all of their time for the local staff. Also similar things come the DOL. The legislature is the same thing. We clearly have three bosses: the DOL, which pays the bills; the governor's office and his department; and finally, the legislature. All three are our bosses. Most of the guys at the local level really never understand that. And CO's job is to take care of all of that stuff which is important, to keep it off of our backs.

To most local managers, however, the central office was a hindrance. As one manager said, "I don't really know what they do. They are continually asking for reports, reports, and more reports. What they do with all of these I really don't know. We seldom get any feedback on the numerous reports we send in to them."

Conflicts between Career Bureaucrats and Political Executives

Director Sheffield attempted to soothe the tensions and the anxieties of the old employees in the employment service through communications in the *HRD News,* personal appearances, and special bulletins. He also communicated his policies to his new deputy directors and district supervisors. The area managers, who were now under the authority of the new regional deputy directors, were responsible for keeping up morale and for informing the old-line managers and employees about new goals and priorities. Yet there were persistent rumors that the expertise of the old would not be needed in the organization, and old bureaucrats began to feel left out. This was to be a continuing problem.

According to Warren Bennis, "One can succeed in infusing new blood, but fail to recirculate the old blood. Old members must know they have a stake in reorganization or in the new organization."[29] According to his analysis, successful organizational change depends on three factors. First, all involved persons must participate. Second, there must be trust in the persons who advocate the change. Finally, there must be clarity about the change itself.

From the point of view of the old CSES bureaucracy, none of these conditions was met. The old career bureaucrats had reason to be anxious. As a result of the proposed reorganization, they were uncertain about their careers, their promotions, and their professional norms. They worried about the new minority staff replacing them in the hierarchy, about being relocated into ghetto areas, and about being laid off or eased out to make room for new staff. Some of their concerns pointed out the underlying tensions that personnel of the old employment service had about the new agency. Tensions were high because most people felt that promotions were going to go to others rather than to themselves. One persistent problem was that most of the new appointments—the job agents, the assistant managers, and some of the CEA managers—were minorities. Morale was low.

The downtown offices, at one time the central focus of the employment service, no longer had priority. The staff there had been shoved aside, and few provisions were made to make them feel a part of the new agency. Not only did this create problems of morale, but it also created difficulty between the old-line managers and the new managers. With some justification, the old managers were suspected of withholding vital information that would have helped the new CEA managers in their difficult tasks. But because CEA managers were in policymaking positions and were getting higher salaries than the old-line managers, the latter felt the newcomers really did not need assistance—they had been appointed at a high level and should therefore know what to do. This feeling was pervasive throughout the agency and was to be a source of conflict for three years before it was finally resolved.

Another problem of implementation was the distrust between elected officials and the professional bureaucrats. This distrust was based on the mutually exclusive orientation and needs of each group. Bureaucrats yearn for stability; their commitments are to the traditional activities of the agency and to their professional norms. On the other hand, the political executive is usually appointed to make changes; his primary emphasis revolves around the needs of the political arena, not those of the department.

The political executive must decide what to do, how to do it, and when to do it to achieve the desired reform. A program's success or failure is often determined by how much time is given to politics and administration.[30] Appointed as he is by the regime in power, a political executive symbolizes preferred values and tends to adhere to the ideologies of his employer. He usually gives the lowest priority to administration. Management problems often receive little attention after the initial decision has been made about what needs to be done. The appointment of a new deputy director to run the central office of the HRD illustrates this point:

> When the new central office deputy came, it was at the time when the unemployment rate had gone up, when a lot of the displaced workers were on the scene; when the whole thrust of DOL had changed back to let's get people on jobs and the hell with all this jazz about the hard-core and everything else; so he came in at a hell of a time. The director at that particular time was involved with welfare reform; and he was almost giving full time to that, so we never had a time really when the director said to him, "Look, now, you understand that the regional deputies don't really report to you. You really don't run the division," and that type of thing. So it's a combination of things.

One of the problems of the political executive is that he is expected to shift his activities as goals and priorities shift in the political arena. If the governor's new welfare reform bill had priority, then the administrative problems of the division became secondary:

> The changing priorities in our department, which is a part of the DOL system, are one thing that many of our people don't understand. The new priority is in let's look at those chemists and those engineers who are unemployed and let's give them attention. This can be interpreted that you're saying to the brothers in the ghetto who've been unemployed for two years, you know, stop giving them the attention. Let's give attention to the veterans; these changing priorities are part of the system. So it was the timing, it was the attention that Sheffield was not

giving or couldn't give because of his other assignments. The governor was on the welfare reform thing, he was identifying our department to a greater degree than the Department of Welfare to get it done because he had given the Department of Welfare two goddamn years to do something, and he had just given up on them and turned to us.

The old civil servants believed that the new director neither understood nor cared about the function of the CSES. There was a widely held belief that Sheffield was there to turn the agency over to private industry. This lack of confidence caused the organization to lose the services of the old guard. As one former district supervisor said, "I was willing to change; I had so much to offer, but nobody ever asked." Some of the new CEA managers argued that Sheffield's failure to change more of the old guard was one reason why policies were slow in being implemented, if they are implemented at all. The new director apparently assumed that the old guard would not change, even if he would have given them the chance. Not knowing whom to trust, he distrusted them all. According to one respondent, he was correct. "The old guard 'hung good paper,' but dragged their feet when it came to implementing programs; and at times they gave bad advice, knowing the consequences."

Bureaucratic sabotage is an old phenomenon.[31] Seymour Lipset has shown in his study of Saskatchewan that cabinet ministers expected sabotage or resistance to their plans by the liberal civil service. Some of their objections to policy changes were based on the honest belief that the changes would not work. Other objections, however, were based on different values: "A reform which may be socially desirable, but which disrupts the continuity of practices and interpersonal relations within the departments, will often be resisted by a top-ranking civil servant. He is obligated to protect those beneath him in the administrative hierarchy from the negative consequences of a change in policy."[32]

Bureaucrats have the power to stop social reforms when these reforms go beyond the frame of reference developed through previous government activity. Only if the changes are congruent with their individual goals are they likely to occur. It is doubtful, however, whether reforms that governments (or political executives) pledge to carry out can successfully be initiated and administered by a bureaucratic structure with different norms and values.[33]

The failure of implementation can also be attributed to a failure of consistent leadership. Leadership that starts reform but leaves before the task is complete makes the new agency appointees less powerful. This was the case with Sheffield, who had agreed to serve state government for two years and then return to private industry. At the end of two years he had completed only half of his original task. It is arguable whether a short-term political executive can change the course of activities in any traditional bureaucracy. Bureaucrats change during a crisis, but return to their old ways when the crisis is over. As Max Weber has written: "The question is always who controls the existing bureaucratic machinery. And such control is possible only in a limited degree to persons who are not technical specialists. Generally speaking, the trained permanent official is more likely to get his way in the long run than his nominal supervisor, the cabinet minister, who is not a specialist."[34]

The Job Agent: A Case of Organizational Marginality

The major goal of the old employment service had been to place qualified applicants in jobs: any job an applicant held for at least three days qualified as an official placement. HRD, however, posed new criteria for success. The distinction was made between temporary, stop-gap jobs, which did not provide the client with economic self-sufficiency,[35] and permanent jobs, which did. A.B. 1463's requirements that job agents keep their clients in employment for eighteen months, help them to achieve economic self-sufficiency, and provide the necessary supportive services gave HRD a fundamentally different set of goals from those held previously by the employment service.

HRD leaders worried from the beginning that the new state goals had no relationship to the success criteria used by the Department of Labor (DOL), where placements were the only measure of success. Whether the worker was disadvantaged, whether the job provided an escape from poverty, or whether the job lasted longer than three days were irrelevant considerations to DOL. Sheffield and his staff realized that an alternative evaluation system with new performance goals would have to be developed if priority service to the disadvantaged were to be sustained. Soon after the department was inaugurated, work began on an employability rating service (ERS) designed to measure the severity of the employment barriers faced by HRD clients. Through the ERS, credit was to be given to job agents and other staff for the work involved in serving seriously disadvantaged clients. Although HRD hoped to have the new system in operation by 1970, it did not meet that deadline. The delay in designing and implementing the ERS stemmed in part from the refusal of DOL to provide any funds for the project, because the ERS might compete with the DOL's new national employment service reporting system. Thus, job agents and other staff serving the disadvantaged operated for over two years without any evaluation system.

The insecurity of the job agent position can be attributed in part to an attachment to precarious values. Burton Clark has pointed out that social values tend to be precarious when they are undefined, when they are not embodied in existing goals and standards of committed groups. They lack specific normative references, and no one knows what the various symbols mean. Social values tend to be precarious when the position of functionaries is not fully legitimized.[36] In contrast, secure values are those that are clearly defined and strongly established in the minds and behavior of many people generally. According to Clark, values may be precarious in specific organizations or in general society because of the weak position of custodians in the social structure. He also notes that groups supporting a new set of values are likely to obtain legitimate status only as their goals and practices become minimally accepted, when they are seen as being in accordance with the value system of the larger society. Precarious values need intentional agents, for they must be normatively defined, socially established, or both.

The values of the employment service, with its emphasis on placement, made the position of the job agent in the organization precarious. He was the low man on the totem pole. Since he could not win the respect of others in his organization, he became a marginal member of the organization. For the employment service, simple placements had been the goal; they were also used as the basis for allocations. DOL continued to operate under these rules, but for the HRD permanent jobs became the goal. To change the basic criterion at the state level and not at the federal level put the new enterprise into a marginal position and made reforms short-lived.

Those involved in organizational adaptation are clearly interested in doing whatever is required to survive. If the organization must choose one set of values over another, it is likely to choose those values that will ensure its survival, not its demise.

The job agent experience suggests an axiom for governmental programs: without an evaluation system to legitimize its work, no new program will be able to survive. This is especially true of innovative programs. The state's failure to follow through on its new ERS left the job agent's position precarious, especially since DOL's evaluation system did not back up the new state system. When innovative values are not protected or seen as legitimate to outside forces, support will be withheld, and the program will fail.

For most civil servants in public agencies, the political nature of change is a constant condition of their work, and most have learned to accept this. Nonetheless, a political executive can only replace a few key people; he must rely on the remaining bureaucrats to help carry out his policies. The infusion of all new blood is dangerous. Some long-time employees must be retained, and they must be reassured by the new organization. To reject them is to lose their cooperation; the effective implementation of policy ultimately depends on their cooperation.

Under normal circumstances, organizational behavior can be modified and redirected by substituting new program goals, redesigning administrative systems, and altering standards for recruitment. To be effective as agents of change, political executives must have a knowledge of institutional mores, possess some administrative skills, and deal with the highly political arena in which policies are hammered out. Few political executives possess both political and administrative skills. Even if they did, the payoffs are in the politics, not in administration. Is there any wonder that professional bureaucrats distrust political executives?

It should also be pointed out that even a well-implemented reorganization is not an end in itself; it is only a means to an ever-changing end. Few structural changes, regardless of their nature, will offer permanently happy solutions. Our rapidly changing society does not permit institutions to remain static. The common hunger for stability and permanent structure is only a nostalgia for that which never was and never can be.

It would seem that the appointment of new leadership is not enough to ensure the effective implementation of policy. Though the reasons are complex, one explanation might be that top officials want large accomplishments from small resources in a short period of time. Another reason is that political appointees bent on reorganization threaten the security of agency employees. This is especially true when the new goals and policies are radically different from the old ones. Although new leadership at the top is a necessary precondition to innovation, the short tenure of most new appointees is itself a barrier to the very innovations proposed.

The new director of the employment service did not rely solely on structural changes for reform, however; he had hoped to devise a new incentive system that would be strong enough to induce old agency personnel to adopt the values of the new system.

NOTES

1. For example, a study by Jesse McCorry shows the extent of freedom allowed newly appointed leaders. See his *Leadership in Urban Bureaucracy: Marcus Foster and Innovation in the Oakland Public Schools* (Berkeley: University of California Press, 1976).

2. The "sunk cost" doctrine as applied to organizations was first proposed, as Anthony Downs points out in *Inside Bureaucracy* (Boston: Little, Brown and Co., 1967), by James G. March and Herbert A. Simon in *Organizations* (New York: John Wiley & Sons, 1958), 173.

3. According to Downs, March and Simon argue that inertia is caused by the tendency of organizations to refuse to search actively for new ways of doing things. However, Downs argues, whether organizations are satisfied or not, they still scan the environment. See Downs, *Inside Bureaucracy*, 197.

4. *HRD News*, July 1969.

5. As Warren Bennis pointed out about his recruitment to the State University of New York at Buffalo, "The promise to build an academic New Jerusalem with unlimited money and with full support of the president, the chancellor, and the governor was alluring." See Bennis, "Who Sank the Yellow Submarine: Eleven Ways to Avoid Major Mistakes in Taking over a University Campus and Making Great Changes," *Psychology Today* (Nov. 1972), 112.

6. Like Hargraves, Johnson was a black and a former high school principal. The northern regional office was in San Francisco, and the southern regional office was in Los Angeles.

7. Task forces or commissions are frequently used by a president or the Congress to build support for a controversial course of action. For a good discussion of this point, see Harold Seidman, *Politics, Position and Power: The Dynamics of Federal Organization* (New York: Oxford University Press, 1970), 65. Presidents Lyndon Johnson and John Kennedy both made frequent use of task forces and commissions to support legislation to increase executive, congressional, and judicial salaries. For example, see Elizabeth D. Drew, "How to Govern (or Avoid It) by Commission," *Atlantic Monthly* (May 1968).

8. This agrees with Frederick Mosher's findings that only a small coterie of top officials do the initial planning. See his "Some Notes on the Reorganization of Public Agencies," in *Public Administration and Democracy: Essays in Honor of Paul H. Appleby,* ed. Roscoe C. Martin (Syracuse, N.Y.: Syracuse University Press, 1965), 143–46.

9. Mosher's "inside-outside" theory suggests that studies by insiders seem to be less costly; tend to protect the personnel in the agency; and are more detailed. This theory seems to be borne out here. The cost was minimal in respect to employee time. Few people were laid off or fired; in fact, several people were promoted. The task force reports were timely and detailed.

10. *HRD News,* Nov. 1969.

11. Office of the California Legislature, A.B. 1463, Dec. 19, 1968.

12. The new director had hoped that all of the job agents could come from outside the agency. However, a suit by the California State Employees Association forced a compromise under which half the job agents had to be civil servants.

13. This he did through newsletters, mainly the monthly *HRD News,* special bulletins, and personal appearances.

14. *HRD News,* Oct. 1969.

15. For such a treatment of decisionmaking, see Harold D. Lasswell and Abraham Kaplan, *Power and Society* (New Haven: Yale University Press, 1965), particularly ch. 5.

16. Aaron Wildavsky and Naomi Caiden, *Planning and Budgeting in Poor Counties* (New York: John Wiley & Sons, 1974), particularly ch. 9.

17. Pressman and Wildavsky, *Implementation* (Berkeley: University of California Press, 1973), xv.

18. As Lasswell puts it, "The political process is a shaping, distribution and exercise of power." See Lasswell and Kaplan, *Power and Society*, 75.

19. Homans, *Social Behavior: Its Elementary Forms* (New York: Harcourt Brace & World, 1962), and Peter M. Blau, *Exchange and Power in Social Life* (New York: John Wiley & Sons, 1964), particularly ch. 4. In this connection it is instructive to know that Gabriel A. Almond and G. Bingham Powell prefer to use the concept of rule-making, rather than legislation, because legislation seems to connote specialized structure and explicit processes, while in the political system rule-making is a diffuse process—difficult to untangle and specify. See Almond and Powell, *Comparative Politics: A Development Approach* (Boston: Little, Brown and Co., 1966), 132-49.

20. Robert A. Dahl, *Modern Political Analysis* (Englewood Cliffs, N.J.: Prentice-Hall, 1960), 12.

21. Homans, *Social Behavior*. Max Weber in his lectures on politics as a vocation states that force is not the normal or the only means of a state, but that it is a means specific to the state. See also Amitai Etzioni, *A Comparative Analysis of Complex Organizations* (New York: The Free Press, 1961). See also Weber's "Compliance Theory" in *The Sociology of Organizations: Basic Studies*, ed. Oscar Grusky and George A. Miller (New York: The Free Press, 1970), 103-23.

22. Churchman, *The Systems Approach* (New York: Delta Books, 1968), 158.

23. Blau and W. Richard Scott, *Formal Organizations: A Comparative Approach* (San Francisco: Chandler Publishing Co., 1962), 244-97.

24. Seidman, *Politics, Position and Power*, 172. In that book James D. Mooney is quoted as saying that coordination is no less than "the determining principle of organization, the form which contains all other principles, the beginning and end of all organized effort" (169). See also Mooney, "The Principles of Organization," in *Papers on the Science of Administration*, ed. Luther Gulick and L. Urwick (New York: Columbia University Institute of Public Administration, 1937), 93. Others have argued that coordination has costs that reduce its effectiveness. Nelson Rockefeller has stated that the establishment of interagency committees reduces the level of government action to the least bold or imaginative, that is, to the lowest common denominator among many varying positions. In such circumstances, policy may be determined not for the sake of its rightness, but for the sake of agreement. See Senate Committee on Government Operations, Subcommittee on National Policy Machinery, "Organizing for National Security" hearing, vol. 1, p. 15. Charles L. Schultze has argued, on the

other hand, that coordination is best done when it is done with respect to specific identifiable problems on a case-by-case basis. See Senate Committee on Government Operations, Subcommittee on Intergovernmental Relations, "Creative Federalism" hearing, part I, p. 399.

25. Wildavsky and Caiden, *Planning and Budgeting in Poor Counties*, 35.

26. Ibid., 36–37.

27. Ibid., 38.

28. My own inclination is to define coordination as authority without power.

29. Bennis, "Who Sank the Yellow Submarine," 116.

30. I agree with Francis E. Rourke and other writers that politics and administration are not separate. See Rourke, *Bureaucracy, Politics and Public Policy* (Boston: Little, Brown and Co., 1969).

31.For a good discussion of this topic, see Arnold Brecht, "Bureaucratic Sabotage," *Annals of the American Academy of Political and Social Science,* June 1937.

32. Lipset, "Bureaucracy and Social Change," in *Reader in Bureaucracy*, ed. Robert K. Merton et al. (Glencoe, Ill.: The Free Press, 1952), 227.

33. Ibid., 221–32.

34. Weber, *The Theory of Social and Economic Organizations,* trans. Talcott Parsons and A. R. Henderson (New York: Oxford University Press, 1947), 128.

35. Economic self-sufficiency was defined by the department as moving the client above the poverty line; one factor in this determination was the client's number of dependents.

36. Functionaries, a term used by Clark and taken from Joyce O. Hertzeller, describes those chiefly responsible for the active "implementation" of institutions. Used in this way, functionaries refer to activities outside organizations as well as organizational agents. See Hertzeller, *Society in Action* (New York: The Dryden Press, 1954), 200–201; and Clark, *Adult Education in Transition* (Berkeley: University of California Press, 1956).

6

Incentive Systems: A Comparison of the Old and the New

People need incentives to work. While these incentives are usually monetary, this in only one kind of incentive. A volunteer for a charitable organization, for example, may devote hours of work because of his or her belief in the worthiness of the organization. Others may spend time on unpaid community work because of a sense of civic responsibility or because their work will bring them into contact with those with higher status, prestige, or power. Still others may work for an organization because it increases their sense of self-worth to be associated with such an enterprise. All of these incentives are personal, and, of course, many others could be added to the list.

Collective incentives must also be considered. Groups working together for common goals (stated or unstated) can instill high levels of solidarity and group cohesion among individual members of the group. Professional norms also reinforce these feelings. A sense of loyalty to the organization is enhanced when an individual perceives that his success and status are linked to the organization. Monetary rewards may accrue collectively in the form of increased resource allocations to a group that has achieved success in the organization's eyes. The successful group's status may also be increased through public recognition. For public agencies, public recognition may well mean organizational survival and increased allocations.

Sometimes an incentive is directly related to a specific task. (If you do this, you will receive that.) Such a formal incentive system is based on recognized stimuli and responses. It requires clear cause-and-effect statements and the objective consideration of all aspirants to the incentives. But in all organizations there is an informal incentive system as well. (If you please your supervisor, despite state goals and objectives, you will receive something desirable or be able to speed up access to the rewards.) Naturally, there are links between the objective formal system and the subjective informal system, but an employee must achieve success in both to gain rewards from the organization.

Conversely, incentives and rewards may be withheld from an employee who is not performing adequately, who doubts organizational goals and priorities, who displeases a supervisor or questions his authority or knowledge, who disregards an organization's hierarchical structure, who does not follow prescribed procedures, or who ignores the relationship between performance and rewards.

If reformers are to be successful in implementing their new goals and priorities, the new incentive system must be strong enough to supplant the old. We know that the term "incentive system" is complex, and objective promotional incentives are just one facet of the definition. The new incentive system has to be strong on all levels—objective and subjective, tangible and intangible, intrinsic and extrinsic, as well as individual and collective. Objectively, the system has to have clear-cut criteria for the achievement of rewards. Subjectively, the new goals and priorities must be accepted by employees and must affect supervisors' evaluations of those under their jurisdiction. Tangibly, the new goals and priorities have to result in visible rewards that are better than those of the old system. Intangibly, the new system must provide greater interest than the old. Intrinsically, employees must acknowledge the worth of these changed directions. Extrinsically, they must feel that the rewards of the new are stronger than the rewards of the old. Individually, each employee must see reasons to work for the new and recognize that good work will be rewarded and an insufficient effort punished. Collectively, workers must feel that this is a desirable, needed direction for their agency to take.

FROM EMPLOYMENT SERVICE TO THE HRD

Turning to our example, the employment service presented a complex situation because the agency was composed of two types of employees—those who had worked, sometimes for many years, under the old system, and those who had been recruited specifically to fit into the new system. Employees in the old employment service had for years served employers and the job-ready and had neglected the disadvantaged. Professional norms and values had been individually and collectively organized around this system. In contrast, the new employees focused on the disadvantaged and had no strong attachment to the old values and norms. It is obvious that those who had worked a long time under the old system, with its own incentive system, would need much more justification to change than would the new employees. They would need a much stronger incentive system because their loyalties were to old programs and to the professional norms that had developed over a long period of time.

To be effective, the new reward system also had to make deviations unlikely by sufficiently punishing those who did deviate from the new direction. Like the positive reward system, the negative system also had to be clear-cut and easily understood.

A further complicating factor was the shift in goals and priorities from an emphasis on placements to that of serving the disadvantaged. This created confusion among old employees who were accustomed to individual and collective success in a different way. If the new strategy was to succeed, the old criteria had to be replaced with even stronger new criteria. The anxiety produced by removing old criteria could be alleviated only by increasing the perception of self-worth among old employees and by helping them to share in the perception that the agency's new directions were worthwhile. These feelings could in turn be induced only by a strong new system—utilizing as many of the desirable aspects of the old system as possible.

The new agency's incentive system had to be formed around responsiveness to its newly mandated clientele—the disadvantaged. Its effectiveness was to be judged by politicians on the basis of whether the disadvantaged received jobs. Because of this, many of the new rewards had to be collective rewards, i.e., centered on the ability of the total organization to find a constituency despite high employment. Without a collective response, the entire California State Employment Service (CSES) would be threatened. One method of securing compliance, therefore, was to show the old employees that the very survival of the employment service depended on finding a new clientele. This was not difficult to do during the early period (1968–69) because it was a time of affluence when few of its old clients, the job-ready, needed jobs.

Since the new commitment to the disadvantaged was a means of keeping the agency in business, it is not surprising that top agency personnel recognized the desirability of maintaining this constituency; however, they were also aware of the shifting nature of the external environment. Under these circumstances, the new incentive system had to be strong enough to offset the possibility of further changes in the external situation. Furthermore, the expertise of the old employees and the innovativeness of the new had to be coalesced into an organization utilizing the best of both and with a compelling incentive system that rewarded the skills of both.

What is apparent from all this is that Director Gilbert Sheffield faced a tremendous challenge when he set about restructuring the incentive system for the new California State Department of Human Resources Development (HRD). It would have to be forceful and yet appealing enough to uproot years of habit and ingrained beliefs among the old employees. It would require these same attributes to legitimize the status of the new employees as they tried to create new, unproven opportunities for a clientele weary of promises and hungry for results.

In this chapter we first review and contrast some of the essential characteristics and activities around which the old and the new agency was organized. Then we shall compare the old and new incentive system to see what effect, if any, the new incentive system had on the morale of agency personnel. Finally, we evaluate the effectiveness of incentive systems as a strategy for organizational reform.

The Old CSES

The old CSES may best be described as a determinate system.[1] A determinate system involves a fixed state. Its relevant variables and relationships have to be few enough in number that they can be understood and controlled or reliably predicted. Such a system reduces uncertainty and increases stability and security. Stated another way, it requires that the system be closed, or, if closure is not complete, that the outside forces acting on it be predictable. In a system with known or predictable variables, the emphasis is likely to be on attaining the highest possible rate of efficiency.

Given the emphasis on achieving maximum efficiency, procedures were standardized, goals were known, tasks were specialized, and responsibilities were fixed. Clients were processed through the system according to an established set of rules, and all offices were defined by jurisdiction and level in the hierarchy. This resulted in limiting the level of uncertainty,[2] but it also limited the organization's ability to adapt to changing environmental conditions.

To achieve optimal efficiency under the closed system, employees were given training in all phases of the operation. They usually worked in both the placement section and in the unemployment and disability benefits sections. They became generalists first and specialists second.

Initial training under the old system was on-the-job training. An old CSES employee explained, "You started out as a Trainee I, and you spent one year in that position. That is the traditional period of time. You were what was called a Manpower Service Trainee [MSRI]—it's now called Employment Service Representative Trainee [ESOI]—for one year. And then at the conclusion of your one-year trainee program, you were promoted to MSRI or ESOI. Actually, it's not different today except that the titles are changed. You still come in today as you did then, as a trainee."

The next step in the process was the placement desk, where the new employee did file searches and referred applicants to jobs. Along the way, the new employee learned how to take an order from an employer and did some employer visiting. After six months an employee finished formal training and was given a specific job. All employees were in training status for one year. During that period their immediate supervisors evaluated them every three months and wrote probationary reports on them. If an employee was found wanting, this had to be established very early; otherwise it was very difficult for the agency to deny promotion after the training period, unless the employee did something quite unusual.

Under the old system rewards to the CSES were clear-cut. Resources were allocated for results in terms of quantity. This emphasis on quantity had several implications for the programs. First, the employer was catered to; he, not the client, was the one to be pleased: "We became more employer-oriented than applicant-oriented. There is no question about that. The system was structured to serve the employer first and then the applicant. You would seldom be real, real concerned about the fact that you had four thousand applicants in your file who were unemployed, but you would be quite concerned about the twenty or thirty job orders that you had."

Second, clients were not selected according to need, but according to immediate placeability. Only veterans were given priority treatment. This was mandated by the Wagner-Peyser Act and reflected the country's attitude toward veterans, an attitude widely shared by old employment service personnel. But even here the service was selective; only qualified veterans received first priority. The law mandated that all job orders were to be held open for forty-eight hours to give the veteran employment specialist a chance to locate a qualified veteran. Seldom, however, was this practice dignified by performance. The pressure on the agency to increase placements by satisfying the employer's needs quickly took preference over all stated priorities. If a qualified veteran was not immediately available, the first other qualified person found was given the job, thus assuring the agency of placement credit.

Third, the kind of placement was less important than the simple fact of placement. "Placement was the priority under the old system. That was it. You were counting them. There wasn't so much concern about differentiating between whether you placed a guy as a scientist or as a janitor. A placement was a placement. Nor was there particular concern about how long the placement lasted either, because at that time the eggs were counted. If you put him on a job and he worked four hours, that was a placement."

The old employment service could reasonably be described as a placement economy. Allocations to the service were based on the number of people placed during the fiscal year. The procedure was simple: people were matched and placed in any job, for any length of time; in return, the employment service was credited with a placement. The more placements made, the more resources the agency received from Congress. The result was that only the best qualified applicants received service.

Job Placement and Organizational Survival. Although the legislation establishing the employment service mandated service to all unemployed applicants, the environment dictated that service be given primarily to employables. Consequently, the goal established by the employment service might best be described as a "maintenance goal" or "survival goal" model.[3] Organizations can be effective only if they survive. Therefore, the shift was intended to ensure both organizational effectiveness and organizational survival.

Placement was thought to be an efficient way to operate the service. Conflict was discouraged, and people cooperated to a very high degree. However, as one employee pointed out, "There was cooperation, but if you want to ask if there was harmony, now that's another question. Cooperation obviously does not, you know, mean that there's harmony among the group. And I would say that the people worked together well, but they disrespected the hell out of each other. They all had a great deal of disrespect for each other because of what they were. They all knew that they were copping out. They knew basically that they had responsibilities to serve the public *effectively,* but they served the public *efficiently.* And they all knew it. Everything happened on time, except performance."

As a consequence of the support given to the placement goal by employees and the decision to screen applicants for the employer, placing the employable was a fairly easy task. One employee put it this way:

Well, I didn't work in placement directly, but I would say that when you're matching people with jobs and they meet the requirements for those jobs, there are no difficulties in placing them. The difficulties come when you don't have a job to match somebody with and you try to serve them in any case. If you didn't have a job, then [the client] would be sent to an expert placement officer, and he was supposed to have a knowledge of the labor market and where employers were and what their needs were. A good placement officer knows how to place people and call and develop jobs with employers without having a job order available. They develop contacts they can use for certain circumstances and they develop relationships whereby employers will take applicants if somebody that they have confidence in thinks that they might make a good employee, even though he doesn't have an opening at that period in time. He will take him and hire him and hold him for the future.

The system was designed to match a worker with a job order in the file; if he could not be matched with a job but had skills, an experienced placement officer would develop a job for him. When this could not be done, the client was out of luck.

As conditions in the environment change, so do the agencies that operate in that environment. New social demands from the external environment are the primary reasons for agency reform.[4] Change in administrative agencies is conditioned upon the conversion of the social demands into new policies. Once these demands are converted into public policies, agency change is mandated. Such was the case in California when political officials changed the employment service to the HRD.

The New HRD

The new HRD can best be described as an open system responsive to its environment. The State Human Resources Act of 1968 mandated a new clientele and required community involvement. It also specifically provided for new personnel from outside the agency to help make the system more responsive.

This mandate introduced many new variables, most of which could be neither controlled nor predicted. The effect of this was that the new agency was more dependent upon the environment than the old agency had been.[5] Its adaptive capacity depended on how well it understood the fluctuating and sometimes hostile demands emanating from this environment.[6] To increase its adaptability, HRD established outreach offices in areas where the new clientele resided. Although uncertainty was a factor, all activities were designed to reduce that uncertainty to manageable proportions, thus giving the agency an opportunity to prepare responses based on a constant flow of new information. However, HRD dealt with an environment that did not fully disclose either the alternatives available to it or the consequences of those alternatives. Therefore, the organization attempted by means of structural decentralization to search and learn from its environment in order to make rational decisions about its future course of action. The new system, then, may be viewed as a problem-facing and problem-solving organization.[7]

Another way to describe the new system is to say that the inputs were unknown and the ends were unpredictable. In addition, the system attempted to respond to a changing environment with the demands and supports coming from several new segments of its environment. It had to respond not only to the Department of Labor (DOL), but also to a new state directive and to new community groups. The decentralized structure also had the effect of giving certain new employees the right to make internal demands. If we add up the internal demands made by its old personnel, its old clientele, its new personnel, and its new clientele, the complexities facing the new system become enormous.

In contrast to the training provided in the old system, training in the new was inadequate. In some cases it consisted of a single day of orientation. As one employee stated: "The orientation was telling you about what [Ronald] Reagan expects and the policies and procedures of the department but really not how to perform you job. People were sometimes brought in and they were placed at a desk and maybe for a day they did not receive anything to do, but usually within two or three days that person was expected to perform at the same level and know the same things as everybody else." Another employee remembered the case of a new employee who had been expected to work with a person recently paroled from San Quentin after a twenty-year sentence. He was to do this with little experience and little help from his supervisor.

Under the new system, paraprofessionals were hired to assist regular employees. This was made possible when the state personnel board agreed to set up a new entry-level classification, one which emphasized the New Careerist concept. This classification was designed to increase the number of minorities in entry-level positions in public agencies. They were to work part-time while completing a core curriculum at a local college or junior college that would enable them to enter the professional ranks at the Employment Service Officer I level. Paraprofessionals took an oral exam and were hired on the expectation that they would be able to complete their college courses in a reasonable amount of time.

The New Careerists were usually members of a minority group. One official said of the agency's early experience with the new employees: "Everybody was bending over backwards to make them happy. They were not told what to do, or even that they were supposed to get to work on time. We had low expectations of them, and their performance in many cases fulfilled our beliefs." Thus, the behavior exhibited by regular agency personnel toward the New Careerists led to what some social scientists have called a "self-fulfilling prophecy." The first group of New Careerists was programmed for failure. As one employee put it: "Some of these people had never worked in an office before, and they needed somebody to say what was expected of them. Sometimes two or three weeks would pass before directions were given to some of these people." This kind of insentivity led to conflicts when the agency finally started to give some direction to the New Careerists.

Another problem of the new system was the lack of trained supervisors. Following the expansion of the system, several people were promoted to supervisory positions, even though they had been in the agency only a short time. One could hypothesize that when agencies are expanding at a rapid rate and leadership is in short supply, the result is likely to be poor performance in the short run, with productivity increasing as people become more skilled at their new position. However, most agencies, given the need for immediate success, cannot afford to wait, and so people are pushed into positions they are not capable or ready to handle. Under these circumstances, the agency is doomed to fail in the short run, and over the long run the agency is likely to be changed before the new people mature.

The expansion of the new system, with its lack of trained supervisors and staff, caused serious dysfunctions in implementing the system. Under civil service regulations, the agency could not contract out for services, except for clerical and legal assistance. Employees in the agency had to be taught their jobs before they could be productive. The use of training resources became crucial, especially as the agency was also dealing with changing goals and priorities. People had to be trained and then retrained as the priorities of the agency shifted to meet emerging needs.

Under the new system the emphasis was on "employability development," and priority was given to those most in need. This shift of attention to the hard-core unemployed also changed the way people used their time. In fact, all resources were shifted to reflect the new priority.[8] The new priority reflected the system's adaptability to new environmental conditions in society. It was a radical departure from past practices; philosophically, it was a turnabout in practice, if not in intent: "Let the truth be known, we didn't refer all that many minorities in the sixties because the minorities didn't come to us. They felt that, and this of course is established in many places, the employment service is not a place to go if you were black, unless you were a professional or you were already in the middle class."

As part of its effort to reach the disadvantaged, the new system not only located offices in ghetto areas, but it also employed personnel to deal with minority applicants. "The new system put an office like this in Hunter's Point with a black manager. It put program resources in these neighborhoods to be administered by the manager of the center to benefit his particular neighborhood rather than having a uniform kind of procedure. It changed emphasis to deal more with the poor people, who probably needed the services of a major department of state government like this one to give it to them in a way they couldn't get it before under the old system, when it was strictly a matter of job-readiness and competition for the situation."

Part of the strategy of giving priority service to the hard-core unemployed also included a rather new practice for the civil service. Thus, some minority employees were hired based on their experience rather than strictly on their ability to pass the civil service test. Although many had the academic credentials necessary for appointment, others did not. The need for people with community experience and of a certain ethnic back-ground became more important than their ability to score high on the test.

Part of the new priority involved changing internal priori-ties as well, from placement to social services, i.e., providing clients with comprehensive services to enhance their employ-ment opportunities.

> Employability should be our primary job in the sense of a primary goal but not necessarily placements. Neither should a counselor's primary goal be placements, but it should be coun-seling so that a person can become placeable or a job agent should be a facilitator for a person to become employable but not necessarily have to place him. If a person comes here purely on the basis of his skill or experience and is placed on a job, then they don't really need the kind of services that could be rendered by the unique kind of organization we have here. Under the old system, one of our clients would have to bring an interpreter in here because we had no one to serve them.

Service to the hard-core brought with it a whole new set of problems. Which of the hard-core were to be served? Although placement was supposedly no longer the main emphasis, could it be totally ignored?

> Let's say I have a hundred slots to run me twelve months. Now, you can go out and pick up a hundred people and put them in the program. And let's say they stick it out religiously, a year from now you might have gotten their average grade level from 5 to 6.5. So he's at a 6.5 where he's still unemployed. His eligibility for the training ends, the program ends, and then what? On the other hand, if you could take a hundred guys with the average

functioning level, instead of 5, let's say the average functioning level is 7, and he's in just as bad shape as the other one, he has no money, he's going through the same kind of changes, and if you put him in the program, and maybe a year from now you have got not only his reading level from 7 to 9.5, but he has also been able to absorb a skill along the way. And out of that one hundred, you're able to get seventy-five of them placed into a job. Now, which group will you deal with? Will you mix them up? Both of them are in the same barrel; they're both hard-core, just that one is here and the other's there. Now what do you do? Because when you talk about having to deal with limited resources in a department that is now result oriented, they want to know what you are doing with the money. How many people are you getting into training-related jobs after you spend this money putting them through training programs?

The above statement indicates that while employability was to be the new focus, placement could not be ignored.

The Old and New Systems: A Comparison

Differences between the old and new systems are summarized in Figure 6. The old system was process oriented; the new system was service oriented. The old system was an advocate for the employer; the new system became an advocate for the client. The old system relied on standardized manuals for direction; the new system emphasized flexibility. The old system emphasized the doctrine of economy and efficiency; the new emphasized social services to the needy. By decentralizing the agency into the ghetto and by shifting more personnel and training resources to these areas from the downtown offices, it seemed initially that the disadvantaged were receiving some services at the expense of the job-ready. In addition, new examination procedures and changes in state personnel practices allowed more minorities to enter the agency. The inclusion of a special CEA (Career Executive Appointment) class for new managers in ghetto offices brought in minorities at policy-level positions for the first time; the new job agent classification also included a substantial number of minorities. With these sketches of the two systems clearly before us, let us turn now to the question of incentives.

Figure 6

Comparison of Old and New Incentive Systems

	Old System[a]	New System 1	New System 2	New System 3
Priorities	Employer; Job-ready	Client; Disadvantaged	Job-ready	Employer; Job-ready
Criteria	Placement	Permanent placement	Permanent placement; Shift to placement	Placement
Rewards	Informal system; Placement; Written/oral exam	Informal system; Permanent placement; Written/oral exam	Informal system; Placement; Written/oral exam	Informal system; Placement; Written/oral exam
Responsiveness:				
Job-Ready	Yes	Yes	Yes	Yes
Disadvantaged	No	Yes	Yes/Shift to No	No
Advantages	Efficiency; Trained personnel	Client-oriented; Policy input Advocate for client	Span of control shorter	Employer-oriented

Disadvantages	No minorities; Not responsive to minorities	Poor training; High conflict; Decentralization difficult without trained personnel	Poor training; No jobs; Conflict between old and new staff	Shift away from hard-core; Emphasis on placements
Efficiency	Yes	No	Yes	?
Success (see text for views on success)	Yes—Job-ready No—Disadvantaged	Yes—Disadvantaged No—Job-ready	Yes—Job-ready whites and minorities No—Hard-core	?
Conflict	Low	High	Moderate	Low
Minority personnel:				
Top level	Very low	High	High; but demoted	Medium; but demoted
Middle level	Low	Medium	High	?
Entry level	Low	High	High	?
Community Input	Low	High	High	Low
Discrimination	High	Low	Low	Low

[a] Note similarity between Old System and New System 3.

THE OLD AND NEW INCENTIVE SYSTEMS

All organizations must provide tangible or intangible incentives to individuals in exchange for their contributions to the organization.[9] James Q. Wilson and Peter Clark have hypothesized that the incentive system may be regarded as the principal variable affecting organizational behavior and that the incentive system is altered in response to changes in the apparent motives of contributors or potential contributors to the organization.[10] Even among HRD administrators there was a recognition of the difficulties that would be encountered in shifting goals, priorities, and, ultimately, incentive systems. As one area administrator put it:

> Well, the first thing you have to do, you have to change the rules, and you have to initially sanction behavior that is different from the behavior that was evident in the past. You have to change the reward system, the official reward system, but in that process you have to keep in mind that it's not the official system that is dominant. In the reorganization, what you basically do is change the official system, and you have very little effect on the unofficial system, and that is the system that is dominant and that runs the organization. It matters when you change the official system because you impact that part of the organizational structure that responds to the formal system, so in a sense you make some changes, but the real guts of the operation is the informal system. You change that by changing the leadership, for example. But in the civil service structure, in the bureaucracy, how extensive can you be in changing the leadership? There are only a certain number of changes to be made, and they aren't enough to really overthrow the informal system.

To understand how one incentive system comes to prevail over others, we need to know something about the factors that shape not only the executive's behavior but also that of his subordinates. The behavior of the executive must be viewed in relation to (1) the agency's history and the era it is presently entering; (2) the degree of dependence upon resource allocations from outside elements; and (3) the political, social, and economic environment that exists at the time and the agency's ability to identify and adapt to this environment.

The question is: How did the old and new incentive systems differ from one another, and how successful were they?

Rewards for Success

The Old System. Rewards in the old system were based primarily on how well employees did on oral and written examinations. Although opportunities for advancement were available to all, those who in fact advanced were a select group. Employees were rewarded only if they received a score of 70 or better on the written test and passed the oral interview. The only exception to this rule was the paraprofessional class; they took only an oral test.

The advancement test for lower-level employees was supposedly objective.[11] The lower you were in the hierarchy, the closer the test was to the work that you performed in the agency. The higher you were in the hierarchy, the more the test was removed from the day-to-day working situation and the more subjective it became. The appointment of people to high-level jobs was based more on their past work and potential ability to manage people than on their ability to pass a test.

The general consensus of most entry- and middle-level employees was that they would be objectively rated by the oral and written panels and that they would be promoted based on how well they did on the examination in competition with other employees at the same level seeking the same promotion.

In reality, the informal system was the prime determinant of rewards. A person could be highly productive and still not get promoted. On what were the rewards based? "Well, that's a good question because in some instances I suppose they would be rewarded for good performance, and in some instances they were probably rewarded for knowing the right people. Probably about 30 percent on knowing the right people, 10 percent on good performance, and 60 percent on how well you did on the examination. That's how the rewards go in the civil service system. In any case, that's how it went in the [employment service]." Good performance meant little if the employee did poorly on the exam. Even if he did well on the exam and knew the right person but was in conflict with him, he would not be promoted.

Employees were placed in the "out group" by alienating their superiors or causing conflict. As one employee pointed out, "A person could fill a thousand places an hour, but if he was a troublemaker, they would say, 'That's where he should stay forever. We don't move his kind.' They would find a rationalization for why that person should stay where he was." An employee could cause conflict by challenging a supervisor's authority or knowledge of agency affairs. Probably the best way of causing conflict was to try to force some kind of creativity into the operation, since this meant challenging the manual of procedures and the approaches used by the agency.

Rewards under the old system, then, depended not so much upon performance, but rather on manipulation of the informal system. An employee had to achieve under the formal system to be considered for advancement, but achievement under the informal system was necessary to ensure promotion. The official system was based on merit; the informal system was based on whom you knew, where you were located, whether you had made any enemies, and how well you were liked by the people in authority. As one employee noted, "The informal system is by and large the one that determines what happens to an employee, no matter what happens to him in the formal system. He could score 99.9 on all formal procedures and never get promoted."

The New System. HRD leaders recognized the need for a new evaluation with new performance goals if priority service to the disadvantaged were to be sustained. The new evaluation system was to include a rating system according to which agency employees would be promoted; it was to measure their ability to work with and place the disadvantaged client. The employability rating system (ERS) was to be completed by 1970 and was to serve as a guide for the new structure.

The ERS system was never established. HRD leaders had expected DOL to fund the project, but DOL rejected it with the explanation that the new system would compete with its new National Employment Service Reporting System. Without an evaluation system to induce new behavior or compliance with new goals, the state's new efforts were in serious trouble. The result was that career employees continued to have to take a test and pass both the oral and written parts in order to be considered for promotion. Again, the only exception was the paraprofessional, who took only an oral exam. Once the paraprofessional had advanced to the professional level, however, he or she also had to take the written and oral exams for further promotion to the journeyman level.

Employees in HRD were evaluated in the same way as were personnel in the old employment service. Their evaluations were based on performance, attitude, relationship with clients and staff, and how they performed the task assigned to them. Members of the line staff had several different kinds of reactions about how they were evaluated. Some saw it as an objective process; others saw it as discriminatory. As one disgruntled new employee in HRD said about his evaluation: "I've been evaluated three times. The first time I had some debate about it because I thought that if a man is already qualified, and if he knows what he's doing, why wouldn't you give him outstanding right off the bat? The last evaluation I got I had all outstanding, except for two. I think evaluations are very poor—they're based on how the supervisor relates to you. HRD plays favoritism. For so long HRD has hired unqualified people to deal with people."

Women were rewarded more frequently than men, and the system seemed to give white females more opportunities for advancement than white men or any blacks. One employee offered the following explanation for this: "Well, women don't cause waves, and they are more likely to remain in a low-paying job until promotion; men, on the other hand, as sole supporters in many cases, either resign to take a better paying job or score low on the test."

Rewards for Success: Area Administrators and Managers

According to Wilson and Clark, there are three types of organizational incentives: material incentives or monetary rewards; solidarity; and purposive incentives—nonmonetary rewards based on the stated ends of the organization. The incentive system used by an organization is closely related to the function of the executive and his role as leader.[12] The executive is the critical variable because it is he who determines how and to whom incentives are distributed to elicit contributions of activity. As Chester Barnard has stated, "In all sorts of organizations, the affording of adequate incentives becomes the most definitely emphasized task of their existence. It is probably in this aspect of executive work that failure is most pronounced, though the cause may be due either to inadequate understanding or to the breakdown of the effectiveness of the organization.[13] Area administrators and managers generally believed that they were rewarded based on their ability to achieve the stated ends of the organization. Success meant survival and possible promotion for themselves and their employees. Beyond this general agreement, the views of this group varied widely.

There were three area administrators in the Bay area. One had the area from San Francisco to San Mateo; the second, all of Alameda County; the third, Contra Costa County. How did each of these men view success? For what were they rewarded? Each had a somewhat different perspective. When asked whether he was rewarded for being successful, the San Francisco area administrator stated:

> Well, probably not. If your bureaucratic program goes favorably in the eyes of politicians, you get rewarded in that you continue to operate your program and get increased funding. That means the more you continue to operate and increase funding, people have more of an opportunity to get promoted, so in a sense you could call it a reward, that you continue to operate. Additionally, if you demonstrated that you are highly efficient and effective, you still can only get promoted through that bureaucratic process. It doesn't reward talented people any more than it rewards the average person. So, to say that you could be rewarded for being successful is that you could continue to survive or improve your operations.

The same employee felt that structural changes had led to improved services to the hard-core unemployed, but, when asked whether the agency was successful, he said: "No bureaucracy, in my judgment, is successful. I'm not even sure they're designed to be. They can improve the quality of their services and the quantity of their services, but if you look at the need and the extent to which that operation is meeting that need, you would have to conclude that it is the most unsuccessful operation that you can find, because they probably only work with and meet the needs of about 10 or 15 percent of those people who are seeking them out. That is because the demand for services and the extent to which that operation has resources is the extent to which it is a buffer between the power system and the street."

Any measurement of success is subjective. Most organizations and individuals wish to be judged on those characteristics that give them visibility.[14] Each area administrator operated according to his administrative capabilities, skills, personality, and attitude, and each judged success differently. All agreed that comparisons were difficult. The measure of success in one center was quite different from another. For example, the majority of the clients in the San Francisco area were hard-core, while in Hayward and Santa Rosa there were fewer hard-core clients and more private agencies and large companies with their own personnel sections to compete with for jobs.

But the agency did make comparisons, and these were based on the same criteria as under the old system—the number of placements made. These comparisons, argued one administrator, were not meaningful; it is difficult to compare areas in terms of productivity because the client characteristics, labor markets, and the environment in which each operated were all so different. In terms of the manpower, Oakland was as different from San Francisco as night from day.

The area administrator in Contra Costa County felt that his area had been fairly successful. When asked what he attributed this to, he stated, "I think to participation. We're back into participatory organizational structure. I meet with my managers formally once a month. We discuss what our problems are, we discuss them and try to come up with solutions for them. If goals have to be changed, very often I'll let them participate in arriving at them." He also believed that his area would meet the division goal for placements as soon as staff training improved. The area had been successful, he said, in reaching goals in training referrals; it had a perfect placement record in this particular goal.

The administrator in Alameda Country viewed success differently.[15] He believed that decentralization had decreased the amount of control from the central office, so that attention could be given to each area office. He further stated:

> I think that in this six or eight months with the creation of the areas, we've been able to go into the offices, we've been able to help identify more responsibilities and prerogatives, set up some constraints, too. We have management systems that can be effective, which can deliver the services that we're responsible for delivering. I think some of the managers feel more comfortable in their own role that they now have. We have established ourselves as a viable entity. People know that we are representing the hierarchy—they know that they're going to be accountable and yet we're helping them achieve those things that we hold them accountable for. I think in that respect I've been successful. I think I've been successful in bringing the Oakland offices back into focus, and rather than having seven offices going in seven different directions, they're all headed in one direction, provided some coordination which means a loss of autonomy for the offices themselves, but I think for the total community, it's beneficial, and we have a place now where I deal with city hall and I speak for the Department of Labor.

Each level in the hierarchy had a different view of success. The employees believed that they needed more training and more understanding supervisors; the area administrators believed that decentralization gave them more power to make needed changes. What did the managers think?

HRD center managers assumed that since the downtown offices dealt with a more competitive clientele and that they had a more experienced staff (i.e., old CSES bureaucrats), their output in terms of placements should also be better. Thus, there was little point in competing with them; instead, the HRD centers competed with each other.[16] The HRD managers were most concerned about improving staff training, so that they could eventually compete with the downtown offices, despite their less skilled clientele. And although competition was apparent between HRD centers, the centers also cooperated for the benefit of the region. For example, if a center was having trouble with an individual, the managers would frequently agree to transfer the person to another center.

In contrast to the situation at the HRD centers, the downtown staff members felt that they could better reach their goals if they could retain competent staff and if there were less continuous turmoil in the agency. Managers knew that they would get their resources if they specified what they were trying to do and if the efforts fell somewhere between medium and medium low. Thus, behavior was based on the desire to achieve, so that the area would look good compared with others.

The lack of a changed incentive system most seriously affected the status of the job agents in the HRD centers. Since the job agents were supposed to be innovative, they needed an incentive system designed to reward innovation to legitimize their work. By continuing the old values of placement rewards, the job agents were not really integrated into the agency. Since their promised rewards never materialized, they remained outsiders, and their work was viewed as parallel to the established hierarchy of the agency.

INCENTIVE SYSTEMS AS A TOOL FOR REFORM

Since the changes in the incentive system from old to new were negligible, the system cannot be evaluated as a strategy for reorganization. We can, however, evaluate it to see which of its factors mitigated against better service to the disadvantaged.

The low monetary incentives of the agency led to a high turnover rate within the agency. Highly qualified personnel often left the agency for better-paying jobs; in most cases they left a gap in middle-level supervision. Men left more frequently than did women, and as a result more women were promoted to top-level supervisory positions. Their conflicts with young male climbers caused considerable difficulty in the new agency. (This was especially true of white female supervisors and black male entrants.) Because of the rapid turnover of personnel after training, the agency was looked upon by some as a training ground for private industry.

Another factor, closely related to the first, was the agency's desire for conformity. At first, innovation was a good word; it later became only a memory that the original employees kept for their own personal esteem. Conformists were rewarded; deviants were not. Conflict was avoided because rewards were based more on the informal system than on the official system. The system, in fact, rewarded talented employees the same as the average ones. Although innovation was supposed to be a hallmark of the new priority to the disadvantaged, innovators were not welcomed, and they left as soon as opportunities presented themselves.

Third, although objectivity was supposed to be the heart of the merit system, it turned out to be quite unobjective. An employee who questioned his superiors or agency procedures might consistently pass the written examination for advancement and flunk the oral exam with equal consistency. Rewards were based more on contacts than on performance.

Fourth, while the agency felt that the introduction of new programs was an important part of its mission, the public did not. The public was not interested in research; it wanted results. For the unemployed, underemployed, hard-core, and disadvantaged, the introduction of new systems or new programs did not substantially alter their situation. Although urban areas received more resources, the outcomes under the new system were similar to those under the old.

Fifth, there was no attempt to improve the feeling of organizational solidarity in the new agency. The different levels of staff had fragmented views of the new goals and priorities. The area administrators were oriented to politics; the managers toward placements; and the job agents toward providing the hard-core with training, services, and jobs. Since the new goals and priorities of the agency were not legitimized by rewards, the agency suffered from a lack of cohesive purpose.

By manipulating the incentive system, the executive should be able to alter employee behavior. His strategy must take into account, however, both the past and the present realities of the agency, the way resources are allocated and by whom, and, finally, the existing external environment. The most significant fact about the use of incentives by an executive is that a change in the rules does not always mean a change in the game. The behavior of employees cannot be altered by changing only the formal reward system. In most public agencies the informal system is the dominant factor determining who gets rewarded. To alter the formal reward system without altering the informal one is to misperceive behavior in organizations. To alter neither is to doom the chances of changing the goals and priorities of the agency, and with them the work habits and aspirations of its staff and the hopes of its clientele. This is precisely what happened in the great California experiment with the Department of Human Resources Development.

NOTES

1. Alvin Gouldner has specified two models underlying the literature on organizations; he labels them the "rational model" and the "natural system model." See Gouldner, "Organizational Analysis," in *Sociology Today: Problems and Prospects,* ed. Robert K. Merton et al. (New York: Basic Books, 1959). James Thompson elaborated upon the natural model by adding the closed-system strategy; he has also discussed determinate systems. See his *Organizations in Action* (New York: McGraw Hill Co., 1967), 4.

2. Eliminating the cutting edge of uncertainty is a major task of all organizations. See Thompson, *Organizations in Action,* 9.

3. Amitai Etzioni provides an excellent discussion and critique of various goal models used by organizational analysts in his "Two Approaches to Organizational Analysis: A Critique and a Suggestion," in *The Sociology of Organizations: Basic Studies,* ed. Oscar Grusky and George A. Miller (New York: The Free Press, 1970), 215–25.

4. This same hypothesis was made by David Easton in "The Analysis of Political Systems," in *American Government,* ed. Peter Woll, 3d ed. (Boston: Little, Brown and Co., 1962), 13.

5. This view of organization as a unit in interaction with its environment is forcefully expressed by Chester Barnard in *The Functions of the Executive* (Cambridge, Mass.: Harvard University Press, 1938).

6. See Philip Selznick, *TVA and The Grass Roots* (Berkeley: University of California Press, 1949), and Burton Clark, *Adult Education in Transition* (Berkeley: University of California Press, 1956).

7. This view of organizations is suggested by Herbert Simon in *Administrative Behavior,* 2d ed. (New York: Macmillan Co., 1957),

and in James G. March and Herbert Simon, *Organizations* (New York: John Wiley & Sons, 1958). Also see Richard M. Cyert and James G. March, *A Behavioral Theory of the Firm* (Englewood Cliffs, N.J.: Prentice-Hall, 1963).

8. The term resources is used here in its broadest sense to reflect personnel, money, and time.

9. A classic description of the incentive system is in Barnard, *Functions of the Executive*, ch. 11, "The Economy of Incentives." Additional theoretical developments and illustrations can be found in March and Simon, *Organizations*.

10. Wilson and Clark, "Incentive Systems: A Theory of Organizations," *Administrative Science Quarterly*, 8 (1961), 130–66.

11. All employment service employees under the old system had to take the entry-level professional aptitude test to advance to the professional class. This test was considered biased, and a new test was created for minorities. The exclusion of cultural items on state civil service tests came after repeated attacks by civil rights groups and others who stated that these tests discriminated against minority groups. For a more detailed discussion of this problem, see Frank Thompson, *The Politics of Public Personnel Policy in a Core City* (Berkeley: University of California Press, 1976).

12. Wilson and Clark, "Incentive Systems," 134–35.

13. Barnard, *Functions of the Executive*, 139.

14. James Thompson, among others, argues that complex organizations are most alert to (and emphasize scoring on) those criteria that are most visible to important task-environment elements. See *Organizations in Action*, 90.

15. Self-evaluation by each area administrator did not seem to be based on social reference groups, i.e., they did not compare themselves to each other. This is somewhat contrary to the findings by Herbert Hyman and Robert Merton, who developed the concept of reference groups. They state that individuals compare themselves with others in the same social group. See Hyman, "The Psychology of Status," *Archives of Psychology*, 2d ser., 38 (1942), and Merton, "The Role-Set: Problems in Sociological Theory," *British Journal of Sociology*, 8 (June 1957), 106–120

16. This would seem to confirm the theory proposed by Hyman and Merton on the use of social reference groups by agencies and individuals. See Hyman, "Psychology of Status," and Merton, "Role-Set."

7
Political Implications
of Bureaucratic Reform

Bureaucracy must be viewed as part of the technology of modern life. It is a way of organizing human efforts to achieve optimal efficiency. Just as there is a fear that the machines people construct may get out of control and turn from being the ruled into the ruler, so there is also apprehension that the organizations people develop to achieve societal goals may eventually become powerful enough to set goals of their own. The conservative point of view contends that all agencies try to assume a controlling voice over governmental decisions. This fear is in opposition to the liberals' attitude toward bureaucracy, which claims that bureaucrats are timid, unimaginative, and reluctant to make decisions.

Bureaucrats are neither power-hungry nor timid. Most are pragmatic and seek to reduce their anxieties and uncertainties by gaining some measure of control over the people and institutional processes that govern their lives. But the means of that control lies in other people's hands. The bureaucracy's dependence on the executive and legislative branches of government links it inextricably to the political process. Quite frequently, bureaucrats' ability to survive depends not so much on what they have done, as on what politicians may wish them to do in the future.

Since public agencies normally come under the jurisdiction of politicians, they are vulnerable to political and socioeconomic changes in the environment. As priorities change, the bureaucracy will be asked to adapt. A bureaucracy is elastic; it will stretch to admit new values when it must, but it will contract and reject new values when it can. Bureaucracies are open to change, but that change is limited.

One inescapable conclusion to be drawn from all of this is: Bureaucracies do change, but they tend to return to a state that is similar to the original one. Radical change may shake them but will seldom break them. When a bureau is reorganized, it will normally go through three phases—innovation, consolidation, and reversion. As the environment stabilizes, the new organization will closely resemble the old.

Reform operates in cycles, but it is difficult to predict the time span of a cycle. At the beginning of the cycle, innovations will be proposed, and some will be accepted; others will be either rejected or put on hold for possible use at a later date. In time, the accepted innovations will be consolidated with the old structures and processes; those innovations that survive will become part of the prevailing value system while those that were rejected will be perceived as alien. Reversion returns the agency to a semblance of its old form and procedures. In reversion, most co-opted personnel who have been socialized to the new norms of the agency will be retained; others will be demoted or encouraged to resign. Pressure and isolation may be used to force the deviant employee to give serious consideration to his or her future within the bureaucracy.

Bureaucratic reform is not a panacea for most organizational ills. Most problems stem from flaws in the policymaking process, and that process is not affected by reorganization. Reorganization has an entirely different function: It is used by politicians and administrators to gain control over policies and programs previously controlled by others. It may be used to remove an unpopular official or eliminate a poorly run program. It is best perceived as a political process for making planned and selective changes in an organization's structure, policies, and relationships. These planned changes redistribute power to new groups and enable the organization to adapt to new purposes.

But reform is still one of the most powerful tools that policymakers have for implementing new policies or programs. In today's society it is difficult to eliminate most large organizations, for so many have a vested interest in their continued existence. President Ronald Reagan's attempts to abolish the departments of education and energy, if successful, might well reverse this trend. It is almost equally difficult to establish new organizations. Thus, policymakers are increasingly confronted with the need to stimulate innovations within existing organizations. Strategies for reform from within include alterations in bureaucratic structure such as increased professionalization, a looser, less tidy structure, decentralization, freer communications, rotation of assignments, recruitment of new personnel, and modifications in the incentive system.

Earlier chapters of this book have discussed the effectiveness of each of these alternatives in achieving bureaucratic reform of the California State Employment Service. We found that politicians were successful in achieving reforms in internal administrative operations and procedures, but unsuccessful in reforming the external environment. Our analysis also showed the following points.

1. Reforms are political; powerful elected state politicians gained control over the employment service as well as the use of federal funds to pursue state initiatives.

2. Reform not only led to shifts in the power relations between federal and state officials but also resulted in changes in internal authority patterns.

3. Structural changes made the employment service more responsive to minority applicants in the short run, but the pattern was reversed as priorities changed.

4. Priority for placement was shifted to the minority job-ready; priority for training went to the hard-core unemployed.

5. Reform of the employment service led to an expansion of job opportunities, and many old personnel were promoted, thereby reducing conflict and morale problems in the new agency.

6. Reform also led to changes in the agency's traditional clientele and expanded the agency's jurisdiction.

7. In the early stages of reform resistance by career bureaucrats was limited because of the bipartisan support of state elected leaders for the changes.

8. Perhaps the most important result of the reform efforts was the resultant agency integration. Minority recruitment for positions at the top, middle, and lower levels served multiple purposes: it made the agency a "model employer"; it served as an employer itself; and it used minority employees to help diffuse the demands being generated by hostile community groups.

9. Employers were induced to hire qualified minorities by using the hard-core unemployed as bargaining products.

The reforms had negative consequences as well. First, the recruitment of new personnel led to conflicts between this group and career officials, especially in the case of the job agent. Second, the new incentive system was not strong enough to offset the old criteria for advancement. And while the formal system was altered, the informal system was not sufficiently disrupted, so that the old criteria prevailed over the new. Third, the addition of a new clientele (the disadvantaged) put the employment service in conflict with other agencies (notably the Office of Economic Opportunity). Incompatible demands and the competition for resources led to delays and caused dysfunctions in agency operations. The agency was also faced with changing national priorities that limited any sustained effort on behalf of its new clients.

The major problem, however, was the inability of the state to find jobs for the people it trained. This objective failed because of two faulty assumptions. The first was the belief that local groups had the necessary expertise and technical knowledge to carry out training and other programs whose designs were themselves faulty. The second was that industry would be waiting, willing, and able to hire the hard-core unemployed once they were somewhat trained. Program failure is likely when solutions to complex problems are based on insufficient knowledge and faulty assumptions, especially when the agencies involved do not have control over the external environment.

A basic dilemma for public agencies like the employment service is that while they can have an impact on *supply*, they cannot control *demand*. Employers and economic conditions determine labor needs; the employment service can only fill those needs when it is asked. Even though the service offered inducements through tax incentives and by threatening to cut off federal funds from certain employers if they did not hire minorities, the efforts were only minimally successful. Thus, while succeeding in changing some of the internal conditions and behaviors, the service failed to influence the most crucial variable—jobs for unemployed minority group members.

Ultimately, therefore, the bureaucracy and the poor were both pawns in the game of power. Most people in the ghetto had mistrusted this new effort, as they had been victimized so often that they expected another disappointment. Trusting only in performance, ghetto residents were less than surprised by still more unfulfilled promises.

And what of bureaucracy? As the political environment changed in the mid-1960s, the employment service changed its goals and procedures. Numerous new measures were introduced to improve service to the hard-core unemployed. Minorities were brought into the agency at all levels, client advocacy was established, services were decentralized, and information on the labor market was improved. Worse than its failure to meet the manpower needs of the disadvantaged was the fact that the employment service accepted its new mission as feasible, thus deceiving itself and everyone else about its capacity to solve problems it could not even influence, let alone control. The manpower needs of the disadvantaged are met by extensive, relevant training leading to decent, permanent jobs, by child-care centers, by transportation to job sites, and by a society that recognizes the need to develop its human resources to their fullest capacity.

Manpower programs and policies have been criticized severely for what they did not do. Few, if any critics, have pointed out what was accomplished. The fact is that history rarely provides circumstances suitable for the development of large-scale policies such as those directed at the disadvantaged in the 1960s. The failure to find a solid institutional base for these new directions or policies was unfortunate because another opportunity is not likely to come soon. That failure also makes a study of manpower experience in California more than simply a case study of administrative change, important as that is.

POLITICS AND BUREAUCRACY: 1968-81

In this final section we make several observations about the impact of political changes on the bureaucracy over a thirteen-year period. Two important questions are addressed: How does a change in political leadership affect a bureaucracy? What effects do budgetary changes have, and what happens to employee morale as a result of frequent leadership changes and budgetary restrictions? A related question is also considered: At what point does continuous reform of an agency become dysfunctional for the agency and the larger society?

Political Leadership and Bureaucratic Change

Most high-level executive appointees have very short careers. These men and women rarely stay long enough to make a deep impact on the agencies they head. Each new appointee has his/her own management style. Given a short tenure, this means that an enormous amount of time and energy is devoted to reorganization, while more substantive issues receive secondary considerations. The leadership changes of the employment service illustrate this problem.

During his eight years as governor, Reagan appointed a total of five directors for the employment service. In contrast, Governor Jerry Brown (1975-82) appointed only three new directors in seven years. Thus over a thirteen-year period, the employment service has had eight new directors—an average of only 1.5 years per director. Reagan's priorities from 1968 to 1971 were on serving the *disadvantaged* and *veterans*; the focus in his second term shifted back to *job-ready* applicants, better service to *employers,* and placement of *welfare* recipients in unpaid public jobs.

Under both Reagan and Brown, each change in directors (except in the case of two short-term appointments) led to a major restructuring of the agency. Each restructuring was designed to suit the management style of the new director and to accommodate new political priorities.[1] The most radical reform (decentralization) was by Gilbert Sheffield in 1968 followed by Sig Hansen's recentralization in 1973. Another major restructuring took place in 1976 when Martin Glick, a

Brown appointee,[2] realigned regions and partially decentralized the agency; he was followed in 1980 by Patino, who, in response to Reagan's federal budget cuts, again realigned and consolidated regions and offices (to save money) and recentralized policymaking in Sacramento. Each change produced a redistribution of influence among agency employees and caused uncertainty and anxiety.

Although it may seem trivial at first, another aspect of the leadership changes that caused considerable anxiety for agency employees, employers, and the public were the frequent name changes that the agency underwent. The employment service was formally established as part of state service in 1938. In 1943 the name was changed to *California Employment Stabilization Commission*, and in 1947 the *Department of Employment* was formed. In 1969 it was renamed the *Department of Human Resources Development*, but in 1974 it was renamed the *Employment Development Department* (EDD). Then in 1969 the federal employment service was changed to *Job Service*. This last name change caused a great deal of confusion in California because people were just getting used to the new name. The EDD newsletter was swamped with calls about what people should call the agency. The newsletter editor made a valiant effort to explain: "Remember: we are not changing the name of the Department; we are simply adopting a nationwide term and slogan to provide quick identification and recognition of our services."[3] As a result of all these changes, even the agency *employees* did not know what to call themselves, and, even worse, *employers* were confused about how to reach the agency.

The changes in agency leadership and structure over time provide some important insights into the effectiveness of bureaucratic reform. The evidence from this study suggests that leadership and structural changes do seem to make a bureaucracy more responsive—if we mean by that the adoption of new priorities desired or mandated by political officials. If, however, we ask how successful a bureaucracy can be in affecting an aspect of its environment—such as getting jobs for a new clientele—then the response is not as positive. Accepting the priorities of a set of politicians does not mean that an organization will be able to achieve the desired outcome. Leadership and structural changes can be controlled by agency leadership and thus the goal of better management may be achieved. But placing people in jobs is dependent upon variables the agency cannot influence, let alone control. In brief, most organizational reforms are more symbolic than substantive, and frequently cause severe morale problems among employees without improving services.

Second, while leadership and structural changes may lead to a degree of bureaucratic responsiveness, few agency employees are overly committed to any one set of priorities, since those priorities change so rapidly. This is especially true if the priorities conflict with certain strongly held personal values. Thus, the insistence upon carrying out new priorities may lead to alienation among employees from the very organization that they were hired to serve. Such dysfunctions will be evident in their casual approach to the delivery of service to the public.

Program and Budgetary Changes

Bureaucrats are expected to carry out programs mandated by politicians. The original purposes of an organization can be sacrificed to meet new priorities. In the 1960s, for example, the employment service was asked to shift from its original goal of serving the job-ready and to give priority to the disadvantaged. The Great Society programs of the 1960s introduced many new programs and escalated the number of new acronyms to a level not seen since the New Deal. WIN, YOCs/AOCs, CAMPS, and NAB-JOBS are a few that come to mind. The 1970s brought a whole new set of programs, each with its own acronym: CETA (Comprehensive Employment and Training Act); PSE (Public Service Employment); CWEP (Non-paid Community Work Experience Program for welfare recipients); ESAP (Employment Security Automation Projects), not to be confused with ESARS (Employment Security Automated Reporting System); CAST (California Automation of Services Team—to set up the new automated system); and EAP (Employees Assistance Program). EAP, whose purpose is to help people with a drinking or drug problem that may affect their productivity, seems particularly appropriate given the series of changes that have taken place in the employment service over the past thirteen years.

In addition to the fact that people were judged by their ability to master the acronyms, there is a problem with assuming—as federal and state policymakers did—that agency personnel had the expertise to handle all of these new programs and that the resources given them were adequate for the task. Indeed, a lesson learned was that inadequate resources are likely to lead to program failure even where employees seek to be successful.

If the rapid expansion of new programs leads to questions about the lack of expertise, then budgetary changes act as further constraints on agency effectiveness. In 1967 Governor Reagan instituted a hiring freeze of all state employees and instituted a budget cut of 10 percent on all state agencies. The hiring freeze lasted throughout most of his first term. During 1974 the employment service budget was cut again by 21.7 percent, but most of this cut was absorbed by the prior hiring freeze and increases in the unemployment insurance budget.[4] In 1980–81 the agency faced one of its most severe financial crises when President Reagan cut its budget by $18 million. More cuts are expected in 1982–84. The 1980–81 cuts resulted in offices being closed, people being moved to new locations, and a staff cut of 21 percent (710.2 positions out of 9,570).[5] Over the years, most of the budgetary restrictions have come during a recession, and, while they may have been needed to curtail costs, it also meant that fewer clients were served at a time when they were most in need.

The lesson to be learned here is that, contrary to what is normally asserted or believed, bureaucratic agencies are neither static nor stable. Change seems to be routine, and, while it causes distress and anxiety, bureaucrats have learned to cope with it as a constant phenomenon and not as an aberration.

Employee Morale

How did agency employees cope with all these changes over the thirteen-year period? There is no definitive answer to this question, but a review of evidence over the years provides some clues.

One point is clear: reorganizations create both cost and opportunities for employees. For example, the creation of the Human Resources Department in 1969 led to the recruitment and promotion of a number of minority staff and young white professionals who were not afraid to work in minority areas. The creation thus did not help the older employees as much as it did the younger ones. The second reorganization in 1973 reversed this progression somewhat, and some of the older employees moved up to replace some of the younger ones.

In each of these reorganizations agency directors persuaded the state personnel board either to establish new classes of employees or to expand those already in existence. The bulk of the promotions went to middle-level employees, but this also made it possible for people at the bottom to move up—perhaps part of a "trickle-up theory." In addition, new transfer and rotation policies were instituted to improve an employee's chances of promotion. Thus, in those cases where reorganization led to expansion, some people were promoted much faster than they would have been. One reason why agency directors were successful in expanding and creating new classes is because a number of people on the state personnel board were former employees of the employment service.

Another morale booster were the awards given to outstanding employees. This practice was started in 1974 and was given wide publicity in newsletters. These people were not only given recognition but, in some cases, monetary awards, too. In addition, they went to a conference every year with the director to help evaluate the agency and suggest changes in agency organization and procedures.

Agency morale was also the subject in 1977 of a questionnaire sent to over 10,000 agency employees. The response rate was 37 percent for all categories and for all income classes. The results showed that employees rated *job satisfaction* as the most important aspect of their job; this was followed by rate of pay. The job aspects rated lowest were "the opportunity to serve the public" and "employee benefits." While the survey showed other dissatisfactions, especially with opportunities for advancement, the overall ratings did not indicate low morale.[6] These data contradict somewhat the evaluations made earlier, for I had found agency morale to be rather low during the first reorganization.

How does one account for his high morale, given the continuous changes taking place in the agency? The data suggest that employees see change more as an opportunity than as a liability. Another reason seems to be existence of newsletters, which agency directors used to answer employee questions, to help dispel rumors, and to show their concern about employee welfare.[7] Finally, one gets the impression that agency employees have learned to cope with a great deal of uncertainty because it is such a constant occurrence. They seem to be able to balance the negative with the positive and treat crises almost routinely.

The latest budget cuts may be different, however; they are reducing some of the very things that seem to keep morale up: awards to outstanding employees, travel, and training to improve job opportunities. These cuts may well lead to more and earlier retirements and a loss of experienced personnel. They could also result in poorer services to the public. Whatever the case, life in a bureaucracy is not dull, and maybe this is the critical variable that keeps morale at such a high level.

Finally, if agency employees desire change, they are not likely to be disappointed. In August 1981 Director Douglas Patino announced his response to the latest Reagan budget cuts—reorganization and consolidation. More changes, more anxieties, and more opportunities.[8]

NOTES

1. Reagan, for instance, has a strong affinity for hiring people from the private sector because of his belief in the efficiency and virtues of private enterprise. Of his five appointees, three came from private industry and two from the public sector. In contrast, two of Governor Brown's three appointees were lawyers who had formerly worked for the Rural Legal Assistance Program (a program despised by Reagan). The other appointee had a Ph.D. and had started his career in the employment service; he later became vice-president of a small college before returning as director. One of Governor Reagan's appointees as

interim director, Allan Nelson (June 1971– Aug. 1971), a lawyer and a past executive of Pacific Telephone Company in San Francisco, was nominated in November 1981 by President Reagan to be Commissioner of Immigration and Naturalization.

2. Glick had the distinction of serving longer than any director in twenty-five years (four years and one month). See "The Director Resigns Effective August 10," *The EDD Scene,* July 12, 1979.

3. "Job Service Comes to California," *The EDD Scene,* Nov. 26, 1979.

4. "EDD Has Flexibility to Face Budget Crunch," *The EDD Bulletin,* May 10, 1974.

5. "EDD Budget Deficit Brings Stringent Cuts," *The EDD Scene,* special edition, Mar. 1981.

6. "Job Satisfaction Ranks First, Say EDD Employees," *The EDD Scene,* June 8, 1977.

7. Indeed, President Reagan had a newsletter, as governor, entitled *Your State Job: News and Views From the Executive Branch* (Appendix C herein).

8. "Director Announces Results of Reorganization," *The EDD Scene,* Aug. 1981.

APPENDIX A

Job Growth in California, 1979

LABOR FORCE GROWTH: TEN LARGEST STATES, 1978-79
(Annual Averages in Thousands)

State	1978	1979	Change	Percentage Change
California	10,646	10,968	322	3.0
Florida	3,711	3,835	124	3.3
Illinois	5,324	5,332	8	0.2
Massachusetts	2,835	2,891	56	2.0
Michigan	4,198	4,314	116	2.8
New Jersey	3,425	3,538	113	3.3
New York	7,838	8,009	171	2.2
Ohio	4,937	5,036	99	2.0
Pennsylvania	5,255	5,296	41	0.8
Texas	6,012	6,244	232	3.9
United States	100,420	102,908	2,488	2.5
United States except California	89,774	91,940	2,166	2.4

EMPLOYMENT GROWTH: TEN LARGEST STATES, 1978-79
(Annual Averages in Thousands)

State	1978	1979	Change	Percentage Change
California	9,890	10,285	395	4.0
Florida	3,464	3,605	141	4.1
Illinois	5,002	5,038	36	0.7
Massachusetts	2,662	2,731	69	2.6
Michigan	3,909	3,979	70	1.8
New Jersey	3,179	3,292	113	3.6
New York	7,236	7,437	201	2.8
Ohio	4,670	4,739	69	1.5
Pennsylvania	4,891	4,930	39	0.8
Texas	5,723	5,981	258	4.5
United States	94,373	96,945	2,572	2.7
United States except California	84,483	86,660	2,177	2.6

Source: Data in this table and graphs that follow are from the State of California, Health and Welfare Agency, Employment Development Department, *Job Growth in California, 1979*, 17-19.

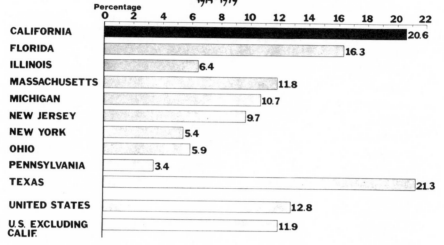

CALIFORNIA JOB GROWTH
(TEN LARGEST STATES COMPARED)
1974-1979

Percentage

CALIFORNIA	20.6
FLORIDA	16.3
ILLINOIS	6.4
MASSACHUSETTS	11.8
MICHIGAN	10.7
NEW JERSEY	9.7
NEW YORK	5.4
OHIO	5.9
PENNSYLVANIA	3.4
TEXAS	21.3
UNITED STATES	12.8
U.S. EXCLUDING CALIF.	11.9

CALIFORNIA EMPLOYMENT & UNEMPLOYMENT
1974-1979

Year	Employment	Unemployment
1979	10,285,000	684,000 / 6.2%
1978	9,890,000	756,000 / 7.1%
1977	9,307,000	834,000 / 8.2%
1976	8,820,000	889,000 / 9.2%
1975	8,460,000	926,000 / 9.9%
1974	8,525,000	670,000 / 7.3%

MILLIONS   □ EMPLOYMENT   □ UNEMPLOYMENT

CALIFORNIA LABOR FORCE GROWTH
(TEN LARGEST STATES COMPARED)
1974-1979

Percentage

0 2 4 6 8 10 12 14 16 18 20 22	
CALIFORNIA	19.3
NEW YORK	6.2
TEXAS	21.1
ILLINOIS	7.9
PENNSYLVANIA	5.4
OHIO	7.2
MICHIGAN	11.2
FLORIDA	16.0
NEW JERSEY	10.4
MASSACHUSETTS	9.9
UNITED STATES	13.7
U.S. EXCLUDING CALIF.	12.4

LABOR FORCE PARTICIPATION RATES

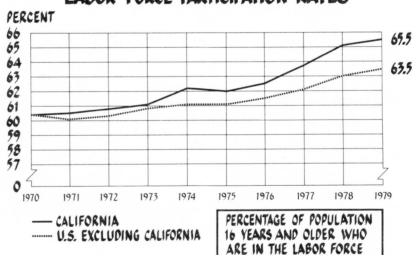

PERCENT

66 · 65 · 64 · 63 · 62 · 61 · 60 · 59 · 58 · 57

65.5

63.5

0   1970   1971   1972   1973   1974   1975   1976   1977   1978   1979

—— CALIFORNIA
········ U.S. EXCLUDING CALIFORNIA

PERCENTAGE OF POPULATION
16 YEARS AND OLDER WHO
ARE IN THE LABOR FORCE

Employment Development Department: Budget for Fiscal Years 1978-79, 1981-82

BUDGET FOR THE EMPLOYMENT DEVELOPMENT
DEPARTMENT, FISCAL YEAR 1978-79

	Dollars (in millions)	Percentages
Federal Funds/Programs		
Unemployment Insurance (UI) Base	107.9	26.0
UI Added Contingency	7.4	1.8
Employment Service (ES)	63.8	15.3
PWEA	10.0	2.4
CETA Balance of State	36.3	8.8
CETA-O	53.9	13.0
CETA Prime Sponsors	14.4	3.5
California Conservation Corps	6.0	1.5
WIN	42.4	10.2
Other Federal Programs		
Food Stamps	2.7 ⎫	
Disabled Veterans Outreach	2.7 ⎬ 2.9	
Youth Programs	4.4 ⎮	
Others	2.1 ⎭	
State Funds/Programs		
Disability Insurance	27.0	6.5
Youth Programs	5.0	1.2
Personal Income Tax	8.6	2.1
State OEO	8.1	2.0
Other State Programs		
Migrant Services	4.6 ⎫	
Service Center	4.9 ⎬ 2.8	
Job Agents	1.8 ⎮	
Others	0.5 ⎭	

Source: *EDD Scene*, Mar. 1978.
Note: Federal programs total $354.0 million (85.4 percent); state programs total $60.5 million (14.6 percent).

BUDGET FOR THE EMPLOYMENT DEVELOPMENT
DEPARTMENT, FISCAL YEAR 1980–81

	Dollars (in millions)	Percentages
Federal Funds/Programs		
Unemployment Insurance (UI) Base	143.0	20.4
UI Added Contingency	56.6	8.1
Employment Service (ES)	83.7	11.9
PWEA	12.3	1.8
CETA Balance of State	50.0	7.1
CETA-O	46.4	6.6
CETA Prime Sponsors	22.1	3.1
California Conservation Corps	6.4	0.9
WIN	36.1	5.2
Other Federal Programs		
Food Stamps	9.5 ⎫	
Disabled Veterans Outreach	3.4 ⎪	5.0
Youth Programs	8.5 ⎬	
Others	13.6 ⎭	
State Funds/Programs		
California Job Training	13.7	2.0
Disability Insurance	41.3	5.9
Youth Programs	6.0	0.9
Personal Income Tax	12.0	1.7
State OEO	127.0	18.1
Other State Programs		
Service Center	5.7 ⎫	
Job Agents	2.3 ⎬	1.3
Others	1.2 ⎭	

Source: *EDD Scene*, Mar. 1981.
Note: Federal programs total $491.6 million (70.1 percent); state programs total $209.2 million (29.9 percent).

Employment Development Department: Regional Structure

APPENDIX C

Message to All State Employees from Governor Reagan

YOUR STATE JOB
NEWS AND VIEWS FROM THE EXECUTIVE BRANCH

Volume 2, Number 7   January 1975

Message To All State Employees From Governor Reagan

In the past 18 issues of "Your State Job," I have been responding to your questions as candidly as possible. Your pertinent and timely inquiries have helped me understand the feelings of state employees, and in several instances I have been able to correct an inequity, resolve a problem, or offer a suggestion.

This interchange has been one of many satisfying experiences in working with you over the past eight years. I went through the evaluation stage that most people from private industry go through when they come to government. I learned that California state employees can hold their own with their counterparts in the private sector or other branches of government. We have been through significant program reductions in some departments and changes in others, and we tried to keep transfer options open in order to lessen the impact on individual employees.

You were understanding in 1971 when I had to defer a salary increase for you in favor of needed help for our less fortunate citizens. I feel the salary and benefit adjustments we supported in the other seven years were fair and in keeping with what the taxpayers could afford.

I was as frustrated as you when the Cost-of-Living Council put a damper on our catch-up proposals over the past two years. I am sure the Attorney General will continue the vigorous challenge in the courts, as I asked him to, to restore your legitimate increases.

I am particularly proud of the new total compensation approach to benefits which we instituted and which was ably legislated by Senator Berryhill. The ongoing machinery is there in order to assure you of a regular and fair matching of prevailing benefits practices. In meeting your short and long range needs on an orderly basis, the State of California is in the forefront of progressive employers. That is where I hope California will stay.

As I leave state service, it is with warm wishes for a rewarding and satisfying future for each of you. I am confident you will continue your excellent service to the citizens of California.

Sincerely,

Ronald Reagan

RONALD REAGAN
Governor

Bibliography

The listing that follows is divided into: Manpower Policy and Programs in the Federal-State Employment Service; Organizational Change; Changes in Agency-Client Relationships; Administration, Policymaking, and Organizational Theory; and General Works, Documents, and Newspapers.

Manpower Policy and Programs in the Federal-State Employment Service

Aubach Corporation. *Report on WIN Program.* Supplement to oral presentation, Apr. 24, 1969.

California. Department of Employment, Division of Administrative Services. *Department of Employment Staff and Funds That Would Be Affected if AB 1463 Is Enacted in Present Form.* Sacramento, May 6, 1968.

――――. Department of Human Resources Development, JTDP Division. "Creative Management Guidelines." Discussion paper at JTDP Management Conference, Asilomar, Calif., July 30, 1970.

――――. Governor Ronald Reagan. *Reorganization of the Executive Branch of California State Government: Reorganization Plan No. 1 of 1968.* Feb. 1, 1968.

――――. Legislature. Assembly Bill 1463 (1968).

――――. Legislature. Assembly Office of Research. *Concentrated Chronic Unemployment in California Cities: Summary Statement.* Sacramento, n.d.

――――. Legislature. Assembly Office of Research. *Subemployment in the Slums of Los Angeles: Summary Statement.* Sacramento, n.d.

――――. Legislature. Assembly Office of Research. *Subemployment in the Slums of Oakland: Summary Statement.* Sacramento, n.d.

――――. Legislature. Assembly Office of Research. "Summary of Case Study of One Job Agent." Unpublished report, 1972.

California AFL-CIO News, 10 (May 31, 1968).

Colbert, John, and Marcia Hohn. *Guide to Manpower Training.* New York: Behavioral Publishers, 1971.

Davidson, Roger H. *The Politics of Comprehensive Manpower Legislation.* Baltimore: Johns Hopkins University Press, 1972.

Doeringer, Peter, and Michael Piore. *Internal Labor Markets and Manpower Analysis.* Indianapolis: D. C. Heath, 1971.

Gordon, Robert A. "Macroeconomic Aspects of Manpower Policy," in *Manpower Programs in the Policy Mix,* ed. Lloyd Ulman. Baltimore: Johns Hopkins University Press, 1973.

Hargrave, Benjamin. "Manpower Seminar." Paper presented at Men's Faculty Club, University of California, Berkeley, July 1970.

The Lawyers Committee for Civil Rights under Law and the National Urban Coalition. *Falling Down on the Job: The United States Employment Service and the Disadvantaged.* Washington, D.C., Apr. 1971.

Levitan, Sar A. *The Great Society's Poor Law.* Baltimore: Johns Hopkins University Press, 1969.

———. *Manpower Programs for a Healthier Economy.* Washington, D.C.: Center for Manpower Policy Studies, George Washington University, Jan. 9, 1972.

———. and Joyce K. Zickler. *The Quest for a Federal Manpower Partnership.* Cambridge, Mass.: Harvard University Press, 1974.

Mangum, Garth. *The Emergence of Manpower Policy.* New York: Holt, Rinehart, and Winston, 1969.

Oakland. New Careers Development Agency. "New Careers Development." Oakland, Calif., Oct. 1968.

Olympus Research Corporation. *Total Impact Evaluation of Manpower Programs in Four Cities. Full Report.* Washington, D.C., Aug. 1971.

Pearl, Arthur, and Frank Riessman. *New Careers for the Poor: The Nonprofessional in Human Service.* New York: The Free Press, 1965.

Reese, Albert J. "Servers and Served in Service," in *Financing the Metropolis,* ed. John B. Crecine. Beverly Hills: Sage Publications, 1970.

Regal, J. M. *Oakland's Partnership for Change.* Oakland, Calif.: Department of Human Resources, June 1967.

Ruttenberg, Stanley H., and Jocelyn Gutchess. *The Federal-State Employment Service: A Critique.* Baltimore: Johns Hopkins University Press, 1970.

———. *Manpower Challenge of the 1970's: Institutions and Social*

Change. Baltimore: Johns Hopkins University Press, 1970.

Stanford Research Institute. *Pilot Study of Services to Applicants.* Palo Alto, Calif., 1967.

Thurow, Lester C. "Redistributional Aspects of Manpower Training Programs," in *Manpower Programs in the Policy Mix,* ed. Lloyd Ulman. Baltimore: Johns Hopkins University Press, 1973.

Unruh, Jesse M. "Statement before the U.S. Senate Subcommittee on Employment, Manpower and Poverty Concerning California's Efforts to Reorganize Manpower and Job Training Efforts and Programs." Washington, D.C., May 19, 1968.

Walsh, Jack, Don Koney, and Al Demond. "Report of the Coordination of Manpower Programs in the City of Oakland and the East Bay Area." Oakland, Calif., Oct. 31, 1966.

Organizational Change

Bauer, Raymond A., Richard S. Rosenbloom, and Laure Sharp. *Second-Order Consequences: A Methodological Essay on the Impact of Technology.* Cambridge, Mass.: MIT Press, 1969.

Bennis, Warren. *Changing Organizations: Essays on the Development and Evolution of Human Organization.* New York: McGraw-Hill, 1966.

_____. "Organizational Developments and the Fate of Bureaucracy," in *Perspectives on Public Bureaucracy,* ed. Fred A. Kramer. Cambridge, Mass.: Winthrop Publishers, 1973.

_____. "Who Sank the Yellow Submarine: Eleven Ways to Avoid Major Mistakes in Taking Over a University Campus and Making Great Changes," *Psychology Today* (Nov. 1972).

Carroll, James. "Up the Bureaucracy: Reorganizing and Reforming the Federal Civil Service." Paper presented at the national conference of the American Society for Public Administration, Phoenix, Ariz., 1978.

Churchman, Wes. *The Systems Approach.* New York: Delta Books, 1968.

Downs, Anthony. *Inside Bureaucracy.* Boston: Little, Brown and Co., 1967.

Drew, Elizabeth D. "How to Govern (or Avoid It) by Commission," *Atlantic Monthly* (May 1968).

Drucker, Peter F. *The Age of Discontinuity: Guidelines to Our Changing Society.* New York: Harper and Row, 1969.

Garnett, James L., and Charles H. Levine. "State Executive Branch

Reorganization: Perspectives, Patterns, and Action Guides."
Paper delivered at the annual meeting of the Midwest Political
Science Association, Chicago, Ill., Apr. 1978.

Gouldner, Alvin. "Succession and the Problems of Bureaucracy," in
The Sociology of Organizations: Basic Studies, ed. Oscar Grusky
and George A. Miller. New York: The Free Press, 1970.

Grusky, Oscar. "The Effects of Succession," in *The Sociology of
Organizations: Basic Studies,* ed. Oscar Grusky and George A.
Miller. New York: The Free Press, 1970.

Kaufman, Herbert. *The Limits of Organizational Change.* University: University of Alabama Press, 1971.

Leiserson, Avery. "Political Limitations on Executive Reorganization," *American Political Science Review,* 41 (Mar. 1953).

Lipset, Seymour Martin. "Bureaucracy and Social Change," in
Reader in Bureaucracy, ed. by Robert K. Merton et al. Glencoe,
Ill.: The Free Press, 1952.

Mosher, Frederick. "Some Notes on the Reorganization of Public
Agencies," in *Public Administration and Democracy: Essays in
Honor of Paul H. Appleby,* ed. Roscoe C. Martin. Syracuse,
N.Y.: Syracuse University Press, 1965.

——, ed. *Governmental Reorganization: Cases and Commentaries.*
A Joint Project of the Inter-University Case Program, Inc.,
Syracuse University, Syracuse, N.Y., and the Institute of
Governmental Studies, University of California. New York:
Bobbs-Merrill Co., 1967.

Thompson, Victor. *Bureaucracy and Innovation.* University: University of Alabama Press, 1969.

——. *Modern Organizations.* New York: Alfred E. Knopf, 1961.

Zaltman, Gerald, Robert Duncan, and Jonny Holbek. *Innovations
and Organizations.* New York: John Wiley & Sons, 1973.

Changes in Agency-Client Relationships

Benson, Charles S., and Peter B. Lund. *Neighborhood Distribution
of Local Public Services.* Berkeley: Institute of Governmental
Studies, University of California, 1969.

Blau, Peter M. *The Dynamics of Bureaucracy,* rev. ed. Chicago:
University of Chicago Press, 1963.

——. *Exchange and Power in Social Life.* New York: John Wiley &
Sons, 1964.

——, and W. Richard Scott. *Formal Organizations: A Comparative
Approach.* San Francisco: Chandler Publishing Co., 1962.

Clark, Burton. *Adult Education in Transition*. Berkeley: University of California Press, 1956.

Cunningham, James V. "Citizen Participation in Public Affairs," *Public Administration Review* (Special Issue), 32 (1972): 589–602.

Day, Robert D., and Robert A. Hamblin. "Some Effects of Close and Punitive Styles of Supervision," in *The Sociology of Organizations: Basic Studies*, ed. Oscar Grusky and George A. Miller. New York: The Free Press, 1970.

Frederickson, H. George. "Introduction," *Public Administration Review* (Special Issue), 32 (1972): 566–70.

May, Judith V. *Two Model Cities: Political Development on the Local Level*. Berkeley: University of California, Oakland Budget Project, 1969.

Administration, Policymaking, and Organizational Theory

Almond, Gabriel A., and G. Bingham Powell, Jr. *Comparative Politics: A Development Approach*. Boston: Little, Brown and Co., 1966.

Barnard, Chester. *The Functions of the Executive*. Cambridge, Mass.: Harvard University Press, 1938.

Berman, Paul. "The Study of Macro- and Micro-Implementation." *Public Policy*, 26 (Spring 1978).

Brecht, Arnold. "Bureaucratic Sabotage," *Annals of the American Academy of Political and Social Science* (June 1937).

Cyert, Richard M., and James G. March. *A Behavioral Theory of the Firm*. Englewood Cliffs, N.J.: Prentice-Hall, 1963.

Dahl, Robert A. *Modern Political Analysis*. Englewood Cliffs, N.J.: Prentice-Hall, 1960.

——. *Who Governs? Democracy and Power in an American City*. New Haven: Yale University Press, 1961.

Easton, David. "The Analysis of Political Systems," in *American Government*, 3rd ed., ed. Peter Woll. Boston: Little, Brown and Co., 1962.

Edelman, Murray. *The Symbolic Uses of Politics*. Urbana: University of Illinois Press, 1970.

Eisinger, Peter K. "Control Sharing in the City," *American Behavioral Scientist*, 15 (1971):35–51.

Etzioni, Amitai. *A Comparative Analysis of Complex Organizations*.

New York: The Free Press, 1961.

——, ed. *Complex Organizations: A Sociological Reader.* New York: Holt, Rinehart, and Winston, 1965.

——. "Compliance Theory," in *The Sociology of Organizations: Basic Studies,* ed. Oscar Grusky and George A. Miller. New York: The Free Press, 1970.

——. "Two Approaches to Organizational Analysis: A Critique and a Suggestion," in *The Sociology of Organizations: Basic Studies,* ed. Oscar Grusky and George A. Miller. New York: The Free Press, 1970.

Fesler, James W. *Area and Administration.* University: University of Alabama Press, 1949.

——. "Approaches to the Understanding of Decentralization," *Journal of Politics,* 27 (1965): 537–66.

——. "Some Approaches to the Understanding of Decentralization." International Political Science Association Meeting, Oxford Round Table, Sept. 19–24, 1963.

Hanson, A. H. "Some Remarks on the Concept of Decentralization as Applied to Administrative Organizations." International Political Science Conference, University of Leeds, Leeds, England, Sept. 19–24, 1963.

Herbert, Adam W. "Management under Conditions of Decentralization and Citizen Participation," *Public Administration Review* (Special Issue), 32 (1972): 622–37.

Hertzeller, Joyce O. *Society in Action.* New York: The Dryden Press, 1954.

Holden, Matthew, Jr. " 'Imperialism' in Bureaucracy," *American Political Science Review,* 60 (1966): 943–51.

Homans, G. C. *Social Behavior: Its Elementary Forms.* New York: Harcourt Brace & World, 1962.

Hyman, Herbert. "The Psychology of Status," *Archives of Psychology,* 2nd series, 38 (1942).

Katz, Daniel, and Robert L. Kahn. "Leadership Practices in Relation to Productivity and Morale," in *Group Dynamics,* 2d ed., ed. D. Cartwright and A. Zander. Evanston, Ill.: Row, Peterson, and Co., 1960.

——. *The Social Psychology of Organizations.* New York: John Wiley & Sons, 1966.

——. "Some Recent Findings in Human Relations Research and Industry," in *Readings in Social Psychology,* 2d ed., ed. G. E. Swanson, T. M. Newcomb, and E. L. Hartley. New York: Henry Holt and Co., 1952.

Kaufman, Herbert. "Administrative Decentralization and Political Power," *Public Administration Review*, 29 (1969): 3-15.

____. "Emerging Conflict in the Doctrines of Public Administration," *American Political Science Review*, 50 (Dec. 1956): 1057-73.

Lasswell, Harold D., and Abraham Kaplan. *Power and Society*. New Haven: Yale University Press, 1965.

McCorry, Jesse. *Leadership in Urban Bureaucracy: Marcus Foster and Innovation in the Oakland Public Schools*. Berkeley: University of California Press, 1976.

March, James G., and Herbert A. Simon. *Organizations*. New York: John Wiley & Sons, 1958.

Meltsner, Arnold. *The Politics of City Revenue*. Berkeley: University of California Press, 1971.

Merton, Robert K. "Bureaucratic Structure and Personality," in *Reader in Bureaucracy*, ed. Robert K. Merton et al. Glencoe, Ill.: The Free Press, 1952.

____. "The Role Set: Problems in Sociological Theory," *British Journal of Sociology*, 8 (June 1957): 106-20.

Michels, Robert. "Oligarchy," in *The Sociology of Organizations: Basic Studies*, ed. Oscar Grusky and George A. Miller. New York: The Free Press, 1970.

____. *Political Parties*. New York: The Free Press, 1960.

Mohr, Lawrence B. "The Concept of Organizational Goal," *American Political Science Review*, 67 (1973): 473-81.

Mooney, James D. "The Principles of Organization," in *Papers on the Science of Administration*, ed. Luther Gulick and L. Urwick. New York: Columbia University Institute of Public Administration, 1937.

Moynihan, Daniel Patrick. *Maximum Feasible Misunderstanding*. New York: The Free Press, 1969.

Pressman, Jeffrey L., and Aaron Wildavsky. *Implementation*. Berkeley: University of California Press, 1973.

Reagan, Michael. *The New Federalism*. New York: Oxford University Press, 1972.

Rourke, Francis E. *Bureaucracy, Politics and Public Policy*. Boston: Little, Brown and Co., 1969.

Schmandt, Henry J. "Municipal Decentralization: An Overview," *Public Administration Review* (Special Issue), 32 (1972): 571-79.

Seidman, Harold. *Politics, Position and Power: The Dynamics of Federal Organization*. New York: Oxford University Press, 1970.

Selznick, Philip. *Leadership in Administration*. New York: Harper and Row, 1957.

——. *TVA and the Grass Roots.* Berkeley: University of California Press, 1949.

Simon, Herbert. *Administrative Behavior,* 2d ed. New York: The Macmillan Co., 1957.

Thompson, Frank. *The Politics of Public Personnel Policy in a Core City.* Berkeley: University of California Press, 1976.

Thompson, James D. *Organizations in Action.* New York: McGraw-Hill Co., 1967.

——, and William J. McEwen. "Organizational Goals and Environment," in *A Comparative Analysis of Complex Organizations,* ed. Amitai Etzioni. New York: Holt, Rinehart, and Winston, 1965.

Weber, Max. *The Theory of Social and Economic Organizations,* trans. Talcott Parsons and A. R. Henderson. New York: Oxford University Press, 1947.

Wildavsky, Aaron. "The Analysis of Issue-Contexts in the Study of Decision-Making," *Journal of Politics,* 24 (1962): 717-32.

——. *The Politics of the Budgetary Process.* Boston: Little, Brown and Co., 1964.

——. "Rescuing Policy Analysis from PPBS," *Public Administration Review,* 29 (1969): 189-202.

——. and Naomi Caiden. *Planning and Budgeting in Low Income Counties.* New York: Wiley, 1974.

Wilensky, Harold. *Organizational Intelligence.* New York: Basic Books, 1967.

Wilson, James Q. *Negro Politics: The Search for Leadership.* Glencoe, Ill.: The Free Press, 1960.

——. "Innovations in Organizations: Notes toward a Theory." Paper delivered at the annual meeting of the American Political Science Association, New York City, Sept. 1963.

——, and Peter Clark. "Incentive Systems: A Theory of Organizations," *Administrative Science Quarterly,* 8 (1961): 130-66.

General Works, Documents, and Newspapers

Bradford, Amory. *Oakland's Not for Burning.* New York: David McKay Co., 1968.

Ginzberg, Eli, and Robert Solow, eds. *The Great Society: Lessons for the Future.* New York: Basic Books, 1974.

Report of the National Advisory Commission on Civil Disorders. New York: New York Times Co., 1968.

Schick, Allen. "The Trauma of Politics." Paper prepared for the

annual conference of the National Association of Schools of
Public Affairs and Administration, Syracuse, N.Y., May 2–5,
1976.

U.S. Congress. House. *Congressional Record*, June 1, 1933.

——. Senate. *Congressional Record*, July 15, 1968.

——. Senate. *Senate Report No. 63*, May 11, 1933.

——. Senate. Committee on Government Operations. "Creative Federalism." Hearing, Nov. 1966. Part I. "The Federal Level."

——. Senate. Committee of Government Operation, Subcommittee on
National Policy Machinery. "Organizing for National Security." Hearing, Vol. I (1966).

U.S. Department of Health, Education, and Welfare. *Social Services
for People*. Report of the Task Force on Organization of Social
Services. Oct. 15, 1968.

U.S. Department of Labor. *Manpower Report of the President*. Apr.
1971.

——. Bureau of Employment Security. U.S. Employment Service.
Program Letter #3092, Aug. 24, 1966.

——. Manpower Administration. *Manpower Technical Exchange*.
Washington, D.C., June 23, 1972.

Index

A Note on the Author

MICHAEL B. PRESTON is associate professor of political science and the Institute of Government and Public Affairs at the University of Illinois at Urbana-Champaign. He received his M.A. and Ph.D. from the University of California at Berkeley (1971 and 1974, respectively). He is the author of *Race, Sex, and Policy Problems* (with Marian L. Palley) and *The New Black Politics* (with Lenneal L. Henderson, Jr., and Paul Puyear). He has written articles for *Public Administration Review*, *Urban Affairs Quarterly*, *Journal of Health and Human Resources*, and *Policy Studies Journal*.

DATE DUE

GAYLORD			PRINTED IN U.S.A.